How to Trace Your African-American Roots

Discovering Your Unique History

How to Trace Your African-American Roots

BARBARA THOMPSON HOWELL

CITADEL PRESS
KENSINGTON PUBLISHING CORP.
www.kensingtonbooks.com

CITADEL PRESS books are published by

Kensington Publishing Corp.
850 Third Avenue
New York, NY 10022

All Kensington titles, imprints, and distributed lines are available at special quantity discounts for bulk purchases for sales promotions, premiums, fund raising, educational, or institutional use. Special book excerpts or customized printings can also be created to fit specific needs. For details, write or phone the office of the Kensington special sales manager: Kensington Publishing Corp., 850 Third Avenue, New York, NY 10022, attn: Special Sales Department, phone 1-800-221-2647.

Kensington and the K logo Reg. U.S. Pat. & TM Office
Citadel Press is a trademark of Kensington Publishing Corp.

First printing 1998

10 9 8 7 6 5 4 3

Printed in the United States of America

Library of Congress Cataloging-in-Publication Data
Howell, Barbara Thompson.
    How to trace your African-American roots : discovering your unique
history / Barbara Thompson Howell.
        p.   cm.
    "A Citadel Press book."
    Includes bibliographical references and index.
    ISBN 0-8065-2055-8 (pbk.)
    1. Afro-Americans—Genealogy—Handbooks, manuals, etc.   I.   Title.
E185.96.H69   1999
929'.1'08996073—dc21   98-42108
                                                              CIP

In honor of my mother,
Agnes Richardson Thompson,
and
in memory of my father,
Leonard Leroy Thompson

Contents

Preface

It has been suggested that if you want to trace your roots, African American or otherwise, you simply have to run for political office. Once your hat is in the ring, hordes of reporters and columnists are likely to apply all the skills of a genealogist to determine just how fit you are for the job you seek. In an attempt to discover all there is to know about you, media mavens will search through court records and newspaper files; examine school reports and look for hidden meanings in your presentations to the condominium pool committee; interview everyone who has ever crossed paths with you or any member of your family; talk with your pastor, priest, or rabbi, hoping to uncover some sin you are atoning for. An eager investigative reporter will trace your ancestors as far back as necessary to find that one black sheep that seems to be a member of everyone's family. An enterprising lifestyle editor will charm your grandmother into admitting that she caught you with your hand in the cookie jar a time or two. Latching on to the cookie-jar story, a tabloid writer will craft the headline: ONCE A THIEF, ALWAYS A THIEF! If you are sure you and your forebears can weather this kind of scrutiny, run for mayor.

Before you take this quick route to your roots, however, you may want to ask yourself if you really want someone else to have all the fun. Simply put, that's what tracing your African-American roots will be—fun! Tracing these roots will also be challenging and frustrating and probably more difficult than anything you have ever undertaken. Still, you will be repaid handsomely for the time and energy you invest in finding your African-American ancestors.

Knowlege of their accomplishments will enrich your life and serve as a source of encouragement. Understanding the challenges they faced will increase your respect for them and for yourself.

The only qualification you need to trace your roots is an honest desire to know more about the people you have come from. *How to Trace Your African-American Roots* will guide you through the steps you must take to find those people—your African-American ancestors. It will show you how to begin your search for your ancestors in your own home, where some of the information you need to find them may be located. Within these pages you will also find information on interviewing relatives and friends who know something of your family's history, including scores of questions that will help you tap into the wealth of data stored in your family's memory. In addition to suggesting ways to gather information from your family, this book tells you where to find and what to look for in birth records, marriage certificates, deeds, death records, and wills. These documents and others like them will take you closer to your African-American forebears. You will also discover how to take advantage of the state and federal resources so important to the genealogist. Finally, *How to Trace Your African-American Roots* suggests ways you can keep your family's story alive for your descendants, and for their descendants.

How to Trace Your African-American Roots recognizes the importance of oral history in the African and African-American tradition. It is oral history—specifically, your family's oral history—that will help you bridge the gaps created when written records are few or nonexistent. This book suggests the most helpful ways for you to tap into, hear, and use oral history. Without your family's oral history, the horror that was slavery threatens to stand between you and your earliest African-American ancestors. This oral history will help you ferret out the slave owner's name, plantation location, or family surname so crucial to your search for your forebears.

To be sure, not all African Americans who came to this country were slaves. *How to Trace Your African-American Roots* suggests ways to find African-American ancestors who were free inhabitants of this country at its beginnings. It also suggests ways to find those forebears who acquired their freedom during slavery, which lasted in the United States until 1865. When the 1870 census was taken, more than five million African Americans were free inhabitants of the U.S. Your forebears and mine were among them. Tracing your African-American roots from 1870 forward thus becomes easier. Yes, it will still require a lot of elbow grease, but you will have more information to work with—information that is, in the main, somewhat easier to find.

Will your research lead you to *the* African who established your family on the North American continent? Perhaps. Some of us have had this rare good fortune. There are steps you can take to look for the African woman, man, or child who was the first member of your family to live in this country. But what if you can trace your forebears only as far back as 1870? Only? Back to 1870 means that your family has spent well over a hundred years in this country. That is longer than many families have been residents of the United States—families whose lives were not rudely interrupted by two hundred years of slavery.

I have been tracing my African-American roots for almost three decades. Some of my forebears were absolute scoundrels. Others are sources of enormous pride. All of them, however—scoundrels and solid citizens—have given me a better understanding of who I am. Our African-American ancestors, despite slavery and Black Codes and Jim Crow and lynchings and segregation and a host of other less-than-civil acts, found their way and made a way for us. To search for them, to hold up their names for the praise and credit they deserve, to claim our kinship with them, is ennobling.

Acknowledgments

With special thanks to
  Hillel Black, editor
  Robert Diforio, literary agent
  Marie Heagney, principal librarian, New Jersey Collection,
    Morris County Library
  David Mitros, archivist, Morris County Heritage Commission
  Constance Potter, National Archives and Record Administration
  JoAnn Shepherd, Bureau of the Census
  Victoria Spencer Spruiell, researcher
  Jane Van Wiemokly, principal librarian, reference, Morris County
    Library

And to
  Lisa Ferguson Dean
  Joseph Howell

How to Trace Your African-American Roots

1

Getting Started

When did you first realize that you wanted to know more about your African-American ancestors? Was it years ago when a friend introduced you to his great-grandmother and you began to wonder about your own? Was it just last week when you heard a young woman gleefully discussing how one of her African forebears escaped slavery by absconding with the British at the end of the American War for Independence? Perhaps you've always wanted to know more about your foreparents but didn't know how or where to start. Whatever your motivation for wanting to trace your African-American roots, this book is for you.

Most Americans have ancestors who came to the United States from other places. Many came at least in part because they believed this country offered opportunities for success and prosperity. More than a few of these immigrants gambled everything they had on this belief. For countless millions, these bets paid off handsomely. Our African ancestors, though, did not choose to come to the Americas. They were bought or stolen and sold into slavery, separating them forever from their families, their homes, their countries, and their culture. If they were strong and healthy enough, they survived the journey across the Atlantic, which could last three and a half months or more. Many did not. Some simply could not sustain life in the hold of a slave vessel, crammed so tightly together that no one could stand or sit or even turn. The hold of one slave ship, the *Henrietta Marie*, only ten feet deep by twenty feet wide, was made to accommodate 250 Africans. Filth, stench, disease, and rodents accompanied the Africans on their journey from their homelands.

Once on the shores of North America, our African forebears encountered new challenges. First and foremost, they had to learn to live in an alien land that offered only the auction block and enslavement. Some, unwilling to accept slavery, chose suicide. Others risked escape, knowing capture meant severe punishment or death.

Finally, after more than two centuries of slavery and a Civil War that lasted four long years, amendments to the U.S. Constitution granted our African-American ancestors freedom and citizenship. Yet there was little time to savor these liberties. In short order the enactment of Black Codes and then Jim Crow laws sanctioned a way of life very much like the one our forebears had experienced as slaves. In time fear of the overseer's whip was replaced by fear of lynchings as former slaves came face to face with the hatred caused by the color of their skin.

To be sure, not all African Americans spent their lives as slaves. The first Africans to reach the North American continent arrived in 1619 at the Jamestown settlement in Virginia. These twenty Africans came not as slaves but as indentured servants. After serving their term of indenture, they were free to engage in those activities enjoyed by all free people. Five years later, however, in the Dutch colony of New York, the children, born or unborn, of a manumitted (freed) slave were bound to slavery. Thereafter, with a speed that was frightening, slavery was introduced in colony after colony in North America. Still, in 1790, when the first U.S. census was taken, 59,466 of the 757,363 African Americans in the United States were free. In the 1860 census, the last taken before the war that would ultimately end slavery in this country, almost five hundred thousand African Americans—11 percent of the total black population in this country—were free.

Looking back from the brink of the twenty-first century, we might be tempted to think that the bad times are behind us. Yet in 1997 the president of the United States felt compelled to put on his agenda and the nation's a pledge to bring about racial harmony. For too many American citizens, the color of one's skin is still enough, it seems, to make life more difficult than it would otherwise be.

Yet despite a history that includes slavery and segregation, African Americans have helped meet every challenge this country has faced. Many have been and continue to be counted among the nation's most talented citizens, some having overcome extraordinary obstacles on their way to success. African Americans have been and continue to be found among this nation's explorers, inventors, lawmakers, healers, architects, educators, musicians, teamsters, actors, diplomats, Nobel prize recipients, composers, generals, writers, sculptors, Olympic athletes, publishers, orators, landowners, preachers, and scholars. African Americans have nurtured this nation's children; served as this nation's conscience; and challenged this nation to live up to its potential.

Many of our African-American foreparents had only their backs to offer us as we climbed out of horrors that threatened to destroy us. Others offered assurance that with hard work and patience each of us could "be somebody." Still others showed the way, reaching back to help us when we became discouraged or afraid or lost. Most important, whether slave or free, our African-American ancestors bequeathed to us a heritage richer than we can imagine. To trace our roots is to learn of this heritage. No matter how difficult, the task is well worth undertaking.

Preparing for Your Search

Perhaps the information you need to begin your search for your African-American ancestors is close at hand. This is especially true if your family has lived in the same town for generations. If so, count yourself very lucky. You will simply have to roll up your sleeves and get to work. Tracing your roots will be more difficult if your family moved from place to place over the last century or two; just locating family members may be tough. Still, the members of your family are vital to your search for your forebears. Many of them hold the keys that can unlock the doors to your family's past.

At some time during your search, you may have to come to terms with the issue of slavery—an issue that confounds most African Americans who set out to trace their roots. If your forebears were captured from the African continent and sold into slavery, determining the port of entry into this country and identifying the people who bought them will be difficult. Locating the plantations they lived on, the families they established, and the offspring they bore will be equally troublesome.

Felicie Young Cormier, who was born in 1879, fourteen years after slavery ended, died on April 14, 1998, at the age of 118. Until her death, Mrs. Cormier was thought to be the world's oldest living person. While alive, she reported that she was the daughter of former slaves. Her parents may well have shared with her information about their lives in bondage.

Of course, no one living today can talk with a former slave about his experiences in slavery; this does not mean, however, that our slave ancestors are without voice. Many of them left records that tell us something of their lives. Some speak to us through records left by others. Diaries, family Bibles, old newspapers, plantation inventories, census data, and the like can provide powerful assists as you trace your roots. Just as important, you will discover that some of your relatives remember old family stories—stories that have been passed down from generation to generation; stories that may help you find your earliest African ancestors.

To know where to look for these stories and other important information you need, find some quiet time to gather everything you now know about your family. Some of the information you already possess will help you in your search for your forebears. Then, learn as much as you can from and about your relatives who are living today. These tasks will keep you well and profitably occupied for quite a while before you must turn your attention to the issue of slavery and the possible impact it had on your family. You can use what you learn from your living relatives to reach back across the years to your forebears. It will be an exciting journey.

If you are like most who set out to trace their roots, you will find answers to countless questions you now have about your family. Most of the answers you discover will be of interest to you, and many will be helpful. But there are three questions you must ask at every step along the way. The first is: *Who is this person?* Is she a grandmother or a cousin or an aunt by marriage? When you know who a person is, you will have some sense of whether she is in fact related to you and, if so, where she belongs on your family genealogical chart. Many families, African-American families among them, consider some people relatives who are not really relatives at all. Perhaps the woman your grandmother called Aunt Bessie was simply a family friend who was taken in and cared for to such an extent that she came to be considered a member of the family. If this is the case, Aunt Bessie is not one of your forebears. Nor is your great-uncle Frank. A forebear is a person from whom you are directly descended. Your great-great-great-grandfather and your great-grandmother and your grandfather are your forebears.

The second question you must ask is: *When did it happen?* It doesn't matter what the *it* is—a birth, a death, a wedding, a feud that separated members of your family, a move to a different town or job. Dates are critical. You must know when an event occurred if you are to find your way back to the earliest members of your family.

Determining when something happened is not always as easy as it seems. Putting the matter as simply as possible, in 1752 Great Britain and most of the British colonies in America (the colonies that later became the United States) changed from the Julian calendar to the Gregorian calendar, the calendar we use today. One primary difference between the two calendars is that the Julian calendar begins the new year on March 25 while the Gregorian calendar begins the new year on January 1. Therefore, dates that occur between January 1 and March 24 fall into two different years, determined by which calendar is used. For example, March 1, 1749 on the Julian calendar (called OS for Old Style) is March 1, 1750 on the Gregorian calendar (called NS for New Style).

Once the Gregorian calendar was adopted in the British North American colonies, the practice of double dating became fairly common place. For example, a marriage date might be written as March 1, 1749/1750, using both old and new styles. When you find an important date (perhaps the birth of forebear), that occurs before 1752 and between January 1 and March 24 inclusive, you may find it useful to double date that information. The practice of double dating may help you understand other information you find. Remember, after March 25, the year is the same on both calendars and after 1752, the need for double dating disappears.

Another important difference between the Julian and Gregorian Calendars is that there are eleven days more in the Julian calendar than the Gregorian. To compensate for that difference, the Gregorian calendar adds eleven days to a Julian-calendar date. For example, in one place you may find a forebear's death date given as January 12, 1710; in another, as January 23, 1710. The reason for this could well be that one date is old style and the other new style.

The justification given for abandoning the Julian calendar after it had been in use for more than a thousand years and the controversy surrounding the creation of the Gregorian calendar in 1582 makes for fascinating reading. You can find more information about these calendars in the *Information Please Almanac* and in most encyclopedias.

The third question you must continue to ask is: *Where did it happen?* Again, it doesn't matter what the *it* is. The earliest members of your family carried out their various activities in particular places—perhaps a village in West Africa, a plantation or sharecropper's farm in the South, or a large urban center in the North where your family migrated to find work or a better way of life. Whatever the activity, where it happened is always important.

To repeat, then, as you begin your search for your roots, keep these key questions in mind: Who is this person? When did it happen? Where did it happen? Ask these questions often. The how and why of your research will be fascinating, but it is the who, when, and where that will make it possible to trace your roots.

If you are to rely on the information you uncover about your family, you must verify as much of it as you can. At times verification will be simply a matter of understanding or thinking through what you find. At other times it will be impossible to verify a particular fact. You may simply have to put verification on the back burner until you have more information at your disposal. Sometimes, however, you must choose between conflicting data. For example, suppose your great-grandmother's marriage certificate says she was born in 1900, but her death certificate says she was born in 1907. Which do you believe? Later in this book, you will find information that will help you make such decisions. For the moment, however, just keep in mind the importance of verifying as much of what you find as possible.

Collecting What You Know About Your Family

As you jot down everything you now know about your family, you will begin to develop your family's profile—those attributes that give your family its unique character. Some families are best known for staying put. Generation after generation they live out their lives in the same town, often on the same street, sometimes in the same house. Families like these are a genealogist's dream. To be sure, stay-at-home families include mavericks who develop wanderlust and want nothing to do with the family's hometown. Often these mavericks turn out to be among the most interesting members of your family.

Other families are best known for the work they do. Generation after generation, members join the family business, perhaps in education, medicine, the legal profession, farming, or factory work. Members of these families take great pride in doing what the family has always done. These families also have their mavericks—the ones who vow they won't be caught dead teaching or farming or tending the sick. The occupations such mavericks choose often add luster to a family's history.

In general, your family profile will tell you something about your family's educational attainment; about its attachment to a given place; about its contributions to the workplace; about its closeness as a family unit. Each branch of your family has its own profile. As the branches of your family come together, these profiles are often altered, modified, and sometimes torn asunder. Perhaps you will discover that your great-grandmother came from a long line of preachers who disowned her when she insisted on marrying a drinking man. If your family is like most, you can be pretty sure that your great-grandmother had some influence on your great-grandfather's drinking, just as he most certainly had some influence on her predisposition to have as little fun as possible. Look forward to the stories you will hear about clashes and compromises between and among the various branches of your family.

In addition to helping you pinpoint certain family characteristics, your family profile will also provide a framework of family names that will help you begin your search for your roots. This search must start with the here and now and work backward. For the moment, let's begin by trying to reach back to your great-grandparents.

Take out two pads of paper. Write your mother's name at the top of the first sheet on one pad and your father's name on the first sheet of the other. Starting with your mother, answer the following questions. (So that you will be able to decipher your notes later on, write your answers in complete sentences. For example, in answering the first question below, write: "My mother's maiden name was . . ." and then fill in the answer.)

1. What was your mother's maiden name?

2. Where was your mother born?

3. When was your mother born?

4. Where does your mother live now?

5. Has your mother always lived in this place? If not, list the places she has lived.

6. List the name and location of all the schools your mother attended.

7. Has your mother ever worked outside the home? If so, list the jobs she has held and where each was located.

8. Does your mother have siblings? List them.

9. List where each of your mother's siblings lives.

10. Do your mother's siblings have children (your cousins)? List them.

11. List where each of your cousins lives.

12. When and where was your mother's mother (your maternal grandmother) born?

13. What was your maternal grandmother's maiden name?

14. Has your maternal grandmother always lived where she resides now? If not, list the places she has lived.

15. Does your maternal grandmother have siblings? If so, list them and where they live.

16. When and where was your mother's father (your maternal grandfather) born?

17. Has your maternal grandfather always lived where he resides now? If not, list the places he has lived.

18. Does your maternal grandfather have siblings? If so, list them and where they live.

Now, using the second pad of paper, answer the same questions for your father; simply substitute the word *father* or *paternal* for *mother* or *maternal.*

Thus, question 2 would read: Where was your father born? Question 12 would read: When and where was your father's mother (your paternal grandmother) born? If your father has always had the same surname, skip question 1.

ANALYZING YOUR ANSWERS

Put your completed sheets side by side. The first thing you may notice is that you know much more about one parent than the other. This is not unusual. For the most part, the answers you have written tell you something about the general characteristics of some of the branches of your family and provide a good starting point from which to trace your roots. Your responses highlight just how much information about your family you already have. They also point out gaps in your knowledge that you will want to fill. You may be concerned because you were unable to answer some of the questions. You need not be: Finding answers is part of the necessary and exciting work of the genealogist.

Following are some of the things your answers tell you about your family and roots. The information is in response to the questions asked about your mother's side of the family: information on your father's side of the family will be comparable.

1. *What was your mother's maiden name?*

Your mother's maiden name is also the surname of her father and of his father before him. It thus identifies a major branch of your family, and may be a key to your past.

2. *Where was your mother born?*

When you know where your mother was born, you will probably know where her parents (your grandparents) were living at the time of her birth. This is likely to be one of the home places for your family. Your grandparents' hometown may also be the hometown of one or more of your great-grandparents. This town may hold important information about your family's past.

3. *When was your mother born?*

We are all products of our time. Whatever information your mother passes on to you may well be colored by her experiences. If your mother is African American and was born in 1920, for example, she may have been forced to attend racially segregated schools, denied access to or required to eat in certain sections of restaurants, or forced to sit in certain parts of buses and trains set aside for African Americans. Her family members may have been denied the right to vote or hold elective office because of the color of their skin. All in all, her experiences may have been very similar to those of African Americans who lived during the Reconstruction era (that period immediately following the Civil War). If your mother was born in 1950, she may have been among those courageous teens who were at the forefront of the Civil Rights movement during the 1960s that changed the direction of this nation and sowed the seeds for the resurgence of African-American pride that continues to this day.

4. *Where does your mother live now?*
If your mother lives in the town where she was born, it will hold important information about her, her parents, and perhaps even her grandparents. You are most likely to find some of this information in church documents, school records, local newspapers, and the town hall and county courthouse.

5. *Has your mother always lived in this place? If not, list the places she has lived.*
If your mother has moved once or many times, you will want to find out as much as you can about the places she has resided. Tracking these places may take you to other streets in the same town, to other towns in the same state, to other states, or even to other countries. Each place will provide some of the information you need to trace your roots.

6. *List the name and location of all the schools your mother attended.*
The information contained in school records is invaluable: It can verify your mother's birth date, place of birth, and the names and addresses of parents and guardians. One of the pieces of information you want is the name(s) of those the school considered responsible for your mother. Was it her parents? Her grandparents? Another relative? It is not unusual for African Americans to have spent time, sometimes years, with grandparents or other relatives while their parents found work or got settled in another part of the country. School records can be used to help verify time your mother

spent with relatives who lived in another state. This state may be one of the home places for your family, where you will find important information about its past. Further, school personnel may provide information about your family that will help you in your search. Perhaps a teacher remembers something about your mother and her family that others have forgotten.

7. *Has your mother ever worked outside the home? If so, list the jobs she has held and where each was located.*

It is not unusual for a job to be obtained on the recommendation of a relative. As a teenager, your mother may have had part-time employment in a factory where an uncle worked or in a shop where an older sister was employed. Early jobs are often in an occupation that has engaged your family for generations. Your family may have a long history of working in education or transportation. Learning about your mother's work outside the home may take you to members of earlier generations who were the first to engage in what was to become one of your family's primary enterprises.

8. *Does your mother have siblings? List them.*

Talking with your aunts and uncles will provide a wealth of information you may be able to find nowhere else. Your mother and her siblings shared the same parents and grandparents. Each of your mother's siblings may know something of your family's history that others never thought to ask about, were not interested in, or simply forgot. Your aunts and uncles may also be able to provide you with photographs and other documents that will help you track down relatives of earlier generations.

9. *List where each of your mother's siblings lives.*

It is not unusual for one or two members of a family to live in the town where they grew up. This may be true of some of your mother's brothers and sisters. Visiting these aunts and uncles may take you to the home place of your grandparents, perhaps even your great-grandparents. You may also have the opportunity to meet other relatives who have important documents or memories to share.

10. *Do your mother's siblings have children (your cousins)? List them.*

Although your cousins are your contemporaries and share two grandparents with you, their parents may well have told them stories about your family's past that your own parents neglected to tell you. Spending time with your cousins may give you information to pursue; some might be very valuable.

11. *List where each of your cousins lives.*

Sometimes cousins will be sent to live with grandparents or other relatives. Where they are sent may be a place that holds information useful to you. Adult cousins may choose to relocate to a place where your family lived previously. Again, this could be an important home place for your family; you may uncover important information by talking to relatives who still reside there. Even if these relatives have nothing new to share, a visit to the local courthouse with its deeds, wills, and tax records, or to the local library with its collection of old newspapers, may help you unlock important doors to the past.

12. *When and where was your mother's mother (your maternal grandmother) born?*

When you learn when and where your maternal grandmother was born, you are also likely to discover where your maternal great-grandparents were living at the time of her birth. This discovery will be exciting: It means you can trace your family back four generations, which is no small accomplishment. Your grandmother's birth records may also tell you who her mother (your maternal great-grandmother) was, perhaps providing your great-grandmother's maiden name and age at the time of your grandmother's birth.

13. *What was your maternal grandmother's maiden name?*

Like your mother's maiden name, your grandmother's maiden name is an important key to your past. Knowing it will take you to a new branch of your family and bring you closer to your roots. If you do not now have access to your grandmother's birth records and have been unable to determine her maiden name, make this one of the first things you set out to discover.

14. *Has your maternal grandmother always lived where she resides now? If not, list the places she has lived.*

Your maternal grandmother's residence can provide important clues for you. She may have always resided in the same place, but it is more likely that she migrated to her current town from some other town or state. Tracing her migrations may provide significant information about your family's past. If she has stayed in the same place all her life, the records you find in this place will be valuable.

15. *Does your maternal grandmother have siblings? List them and where they live.*

Your maternal grandmother's brothers and sisters—your great-aunts and -uncles—grew up with your grandmother, sharing the same parents (your maternal great-grandparents) and many of the same experiences. Their memories, impressions, and mementos will be among the most valuable available to you; talk with these relatives at your earliest convenience.

16. *When and where was your mother's father (your maternal grandfather) born?*

Knowing your maternal grandfather's birthplace is more important than you might imagine. By pinpointing his birthplace, you will know where his parents, your maternal great-grandparents, were living at the time of his birth. Coupling this information with that gathered about your maternal grandmother's birthplace gives you information about four of your eight great-grandparents. When you have answered the questions about your father, you may well have some information about all eight of your great-grandparents, which will give you a solid framework to build on.

17. *Has your maternal grandfather always lived where he resides now? If not, list the places he has lived.*

Perhaps your grandfather lived in many places before settling down in his current home. Knowing where he has lived will help you trace your roots. If where he lives now is his home place, you will find the town rich in resources that will speed your search.

18. *Does your maternal grandfather have siblings? If so, list them and where they live.*

As with your maternal grandmother's siblings, these great-aunts and -uncles can provide a wealth of information about your mother's family. Add this to what you learn from your maternal grandmother's siblings and you will be in a position to compile a great deal of information about your mother's side of the family. The same will be true for your father's side of the family when you have answered the same questions about him.

As you think about your family and its various members, you may realize there are other things you know that will be important in your search for your roots. Write them down while they are fresh in your mind. Like parts of a puzzle, you will find a place for each piece of information as you assemble the huge and colorful mosaic that represents your family.

IDENTIFYING PEOPLE WHO CAN HELP YOU

As you were answering questions about various members of your family, you probably listed relatives you have not thought about for a long time. Some of them will be helpful to you in your search for your roots. Although an accident or illness can befall a family member at any time, you are most likely to lose those relatives who are the oldest members of your family. If any of your eight great-grandparents are still alive, plan to visit them as soon as possible. Tell them of your interest in tracing your family's roots and make sure they know you are doing this just for the family. (Chapter 4 will explain the importance that older relatives place on keeping family confidences. Your failure to understand this may deny you access to valuable information.) Matching your great-grandparents in importance will be any great-great aunts or -uncles (your great-grandparents' siblings) who may still be living: Their memories will be the oldest firsthand accounts available to you. Since these older relatives may be coming to the end of their lives, tap into their memories as soon as possible.

Next in importance to your great-grandparents and their siblings will be your four grandparents and their siblings (your great-aunts and -uncles). You may not have visited or talked with some of these relatives for a long time. Contact them as soon as possible. In the absence of great-grandparents, your grandparents' generation will provide the oldest firsthand information available to you. Of course, your own parents and their siblings will be able to help you, especially those who may be designated as "keepers" or, less kindly, "pack rats." Every generation has its keepers; these family members are the ones likely to have been entrusted by the previous generation with valuable family documents and mementos. One of your aunts may have a grandmother's marriage document, for example, or a program from a great-grandfather's burial service.

Make a list of the relatives who may be able to help you trace your roots. Beside each name write either your father's surname or your mother's maiden name, to indicate the parent each relative may know most about. Next, write down the address and telephone number for each relative on your list. You may find that you do not have a current address or phone number. If the relative in question lives nearby, consult the local phone directory. If he lives out of town or out of state, make a note to check with another relative who may have the information you need. If all else fails, you may have to spend some time at your local or county library looking through out-of-state telephone directories until you find the information you need.

Put an asterisk next to each name on the list that represents a relative who lives fairly close to you. These will be among the relatives you will want to contact first. The only relatives who will take precedence over those who live nearby will be any great-grandparents, grandparents, or their siblings. Otherwise, limit your initial visits to those who are within easy driving distance or can be reached by public transportation. Not only will you find this a comfortable way to start your search, but some of these relatives will also give you information that will help you decide which of your more distant relatives warrant a visit.

MAKING THE HARD DECISIONS

In developing your family profile, you may have filled a dozen or more sheets of paper with information about your parents, grandparents, and great-grandparents. You probably have several more sheets of notes reflecting your own memories of family events or milestones. If you know the surnames of all your great-grandparents, you have identified eight separate branches of your family. How do you go about tracking all of them? You don't. At least not at the same time.

At the beginning of your search, you need to focus as much of your attention as possible on those relatives most likely to bring the best results. Look at your notes again. At this moment, do you know more about your mother's family or your father's? Did one parent's family stay in a given place for a long time? For example, if your mother and her parents and grandparents have always lived in the same town, this town should yield much of the information you need to begin to trace your roots. Remember, knowing the maiden names of your female forebears will be vital to your search.

On the other hand, members of your father's family may have been the ones to stay put for generations. Equally important, your father's surname is known to you, and it is likely the name that he and his forebears have carried for a long time. Even if it is a name they chose after slavery, it will carry you back well over a century. If you are lucky enough to have two parents whose families have stayed put, choose the family that interests you most right now or toss a coin to decide with which family you will begin.

When I began my own search for roots, I knew something about my father's family and virtually nothing about my mother's. It was not difficult to decide to trace my roots through the Thompson line. I must admit that I was also intrigued with my Thompson roots because, as far as I knew, none of my Thompson forebears had been born south of the Mason-Dixon line. (All my African-American friends and acquaintances have some ties to the South. I am still looking for the Thompsons' southern connection. It may well be that there is none. As early as 1624, while this country was still under British rule, African Americans were living in the North.) Concentrating on just the Thompsons, I found a large and interesting group of ancestors. Among them are four teamsters (one of whom drove a horse and buggy for Standard Oil), a Buffalo Soldier, two farmers, a logger, dozens of property owners, three musicians, and more than a few hell-raisers (one of whom was directly responsible for the destruction of family documents that the Thompsons had saved for generations—but more about this later).

Of course, not everyone I found was a Thompson. My Thompson genealogy chart includes Richardsons, Conovers, Williamses, Andersons, and Oakeses, all of whom represent people connected to the Thompsons through marriage. So concentrating on just one parent does not mean that you will be dealing with only one surname. Nor do you ever have to worry about running out of people to research. You know you have four grandparents and eight great-grandparents. You also have sixteen great-great-grandparents and thirty-two great-great-great-grandparents. If you trace your direct forebears back through ten generations, you will find that you have 1,024 of them. With work, effort, and luck, you may be able to track ten generations of one or more branches of your family. You will be most successful in doing this, however, if you start with the here and now. Even if you know something about a forebear who was born in 1820, it will be wiser and easier to start your search for your African-American roots with the mother or father who was born in 1930 and work your way back to that 1820 forebear. To do otherwise may cause you to miss important clues that will help you link today with the past.

Thus far, you've thought about some of the problems African Americans face in tracing their roots and attempted to trace your own family back to your eight great-grandparents. You've also made a list of relatives who may be able to help you learn more about your ancestors, including their addresses and telephone numbers. Before you begin to trace your roots, however, give some thought to how you will keep track of everything you learn about your family. Make no mistake about it, there will be a lot to keep track of. Record keeping is an issue you will have to deal with sooner or later and, in this instance, sooner is better. The next chapter will suggest ways to keep track of all the information you uncover while looking for your earliest African-American ancestors.

2

Keeping Track of Everything

Right now you may be looking at all those pieces of paper you generated simply by answering a few questions about your parents. The first thing you need to do is get this information a little better organized so that it will be of use to you in your search for your roots. One way to do so is to put the information into folders. For the moment, you will need just four. These folders are simply temporary holding places; ultimately, much of the data you will store in them will be placed in research notebooks filled with Individual Family Worksheets, or whatever forms you choose to use. (Both research notebooks and Individual Family Worksheets will be discussed later in this chapter.)

Put the information you recorded about your mother and her family in one folder and label it with your mother's maiden name—for example, JOHNSON. The information about your father will be put in a second folder labeled with his surname—perhaps WRIGHT. The list of family and friends who may be able to help in your search will be put in the third folder and labeled FAMILY RESOURCES; keep your own notes and recollections in the fourth folder, GENERAL.

Look at the list of names in the FAMILY RESOURCES folder. Next to some of these names you have put either your mother's maiden name or your father's surname. Now you need to separate them. On one sheet of paper, make a list of the names, addresses, and telephone numbers of the people you believe will be able to help you learn more about your mother's family. Perhaps the list will include your mother's mother (your grandmother), four of her siblings (your aunts and uncles), three of her aunts (your great-aunts), two uncles (your great-uncles), several cousins (your second cousins), the minister of the church where she was married, one or two of her schoolteachers, and a lifelong friend with whom she talks several times a week.

On a second sheet of paper, copy the names, addresses, and telephone numbers of those who can help you search for your roots through your father's family. Title your mother's list with her maiden name and then the words *People Resources*—for example, JOHNSON PEOPLE RESOURCES. (Your father's list would of course be titled similarly, using his surname.) Put each list in the appropriate parent's folder. Recopy any names that remain on the original list. Put this revised list in the FAMILY RESOURCES folder until you know whether those listed will help you learn more about your mother or your father. When you know, transfer the names to the appropriate parent's folder.

You may wonder why I have suggested you label your list JOHN-SON PEOPLE RESOURCES. During your search for your roots, you will be exploring many kinds of resources, only some of which will be people. You can, of course, label any list any way you like. Just be sure the label you use lets you know what the list contains. Proper labeling is a time-saving device that you will come to appreciate as the volume of the data you collect increases.

GATHERING SUPPLIES TO ORGANIZE YOUR SEARCH

Tracing your African-American roots is a significant undertaking. As with any major project, you will need some general supplies to help you organize the work at hand. Those you need to carry out your genealogical activities are easy to acquire and can be fairly inexpensive: three-ring binders that will serve as research notebooks; ballpoint pens; a file cabinet or cardboard filing box; file cabinet folders and hangers; nine- by seventen-inch manila folders; a battery-powered tape recorder; and an inexpensive camera.

Research Notebooks

As you undertake your search for your earliest African ancestors, one of your primary tools will be a three-ring binder or notebook that holds eight-and-a-half by eleven-inch paper. You will also need notebook dividers so that you can separate your notebook into sections, and of course notebook paper. Many find that lined paper is easiest to use. A single notebook should be used exclusively for the family that you have chosen to begin your search with (either your mother's or your father's). If you have decided to search for both families simultaneously, you will need two notebooks because, as I mentioned earlier, a single surname will lead to many others.

Use notebook dividers to separate your research notebook into these sections: genealogical charts; Individual Family Worksheets; birth records; marriage records; death records; school records; and military records. The genealogical charts in each notebook will pertain to the family the notebook covers. These charts will serve as your road map, keeping you on track. (You will find information about genealogical charts and Individual Family Worksheets later in this chapter.)

Put ten or fifteen sheets of blank paper after each divider. On these sheets of paper you can record information you find about a given subject, or perhaps paste in copies of documents you have found so that you can refer to them whenever necessary. The importance of having copies of documents to refer to will become obvious as you begin to discover the wealth of information a single document can contain. (Never put original documents in your notebook. Original marriage certificates, deeds, and the like are irreplaceable and every effort should be made to keep them in a safe place and as near their original condition as possible.)

Buy a good supply of inexpensive ballpoint pens to record information in your research notebooks. (As surprising as it may seem, pencil sharpeners are not always available at research sites.) Be sure you can read the notes you take—sometimes easier said than done. There have been times when I was so excited by information I discovered that my notes were virtually illegible the next day. I learned to check legibility before leaving a research site. Return visits simply to recopy information more carefully can be costly.

File Cabinets or Boxes

As you trace your roots you will acquire copies of any number of documents that you will need to keep in a safe place and have easy access to. Among these documents will be records of births, marriages, and deaths; copies of wills and deeds; military records; old letters and diaries; family photographs; school yearbooks; and even report cards. A good place to keep these documents is a file cabinet.

There are a variety of file cabinets to choose from. You will probably want to begin with a two-drawer cabinet that holds nine- by seventeen-inch papers, to accommodate larger documents, such as wills or deeds, without forcing you to fold them. To use the cabinet effectively, you will need hangers and hanging folders, as well as tabs to label the folders. As you accumulate information you will want to file like items together—for example, putting all records of birth in one place and all records of death in another. You will, of course, organize the items within a given section by surname. The hanging folders make alphabetical organization quite easy. Manila folders placed within the hanging folders will allow you to file like documents by surname. If you don't have a file cabinet and are not ready to invest in one, a cardboard filing box works just as well and costs only a few dollars.

Index Cards

At times you will have unexpected opportunities to gather information about your family. You may meet one of your parent's classmates in the supermarket or at the dry cleaner. An elderly neighbor may suddenly engage you in conversation in a coffee shop, sharing information about your relatives that no one had before. In these situations or others like them, you may not have your research notebook with you—but you can always have index cards available in your pocket or purse.

Index cards are not intended to provide a permanent record but rather to hold information you will later record in your research notebook. Small index cards (three by five inches) are the easiest to handle. If the cards are lined, you will find that they force a kind of legibility that unlined cards do not. To assure that you will transfer the information to the correct place in your research notebook, always write the surname the information applies to in the upper right-hand corner of the card. On the card's first line, write the name of the informant and the date you acquired the information. An example of how a completed index card might look is shown below.

WILLIAMS

1. INFORMANT: JOHN BRUCE

2. DATE: December 4, 1998

3. SUBJECT: PROPERTY OWNERSHIP

4. INFORMATION: *"Your family owned a good piece of property in Georgia. It was near the old Jacobs plantation somewhere outside Macon. Your great-grandmother Bertha talked about it all the time."*

The importance of the information Mr. Bruce provided is obvious. You know it relates to the Williams family because you have learned that your great-grandmother Bertha's maiden name was Williams. If you don't know her maiden name, buy Mr. Jacobs another cup of coffee and try to jog his memory. Further conversation might be a good idea in any case: Perhaps your great-grandmother shared other information with Mr. Bruce that will help you in your search for the branch of your family that owned a good piece of land outside Macon, Georgia.

Limit the information on each card to a single fact or idea. This will make it easier for you to transcribe the information to the appropriate place in your research notebook. Moreover, do not decide out of hand that something you hear about your family is of no consequence. Everything you learn is important, at least at first. When you have reached your goal of finding your earliest African-American ancestors, you can then decide which information is unimportant.

If you learn or overhear something and do not have the opportunity to record the information when you hear it, stop as soon as possible to do so. This may mean finding a park bench, a rest room with a lounge, or a wall to lean against. I cannot stress too much the importance of recording the information you discover as soon as possible. No matter how excellent your memory is, as you collect hundreds of facts about your family, you will need good notes to piece them all together. The one fact you forget may be the very fact you need to lead you to the earliest members of your family.

Tape Recorders

During the course of your research, you will conduct a variety of interviews. If you are permitted to do so, be prepared to record them. Trying to commit everything you hear to memory, or trying to write down everything that is said to you, almost guarantees that you will miss something. Without fail, some of those somethings will be important. Recording the interview will give you the opportunity to review everything you hear as often as you need to. The audiotapes will also be valuable as you discover corroborating information. Further, having a relative's voice on tape—a voice with its own cadence, its own use of language and colloquialisms, its own expression of joy or dismay—is a splendid way to give depth to the information you collect about your family.

There are a great many tape recorders to choose from. You can find one that is serviceable in an office supply or electronics store for less than thirty dollars. A recorder about the size of the palm of your hand will work best, because it fits easily into a pocket or purse. It may be important to keep a recorder out of sight until permission is given to use it. (You will read more about this element of interviewing in chapter 4.) Just as important, you will not want to be encumbered by bulky equipment during your research activities. Choose a battery-powered recorder. If given permission to record an interview, you will not want to have to waste valuable time looking for an electrical outlet. If nothing else, this kind of interruption can be off-putting to the person you are planning to interview. Be sure to have an extra battery or two and several blank tapes.

In addition to recording interviews, you will find a tape recorder helpful in recording your reactions to various research sites. When visiting a cemetery, for example, you may want to record your impressions of the location of the cemetery itself, the location of a particular gravestone, and something about the gravestones around it. With concentration or the help of maps, you may be able to determine whether the part of the cemetery where you have found an ancestor seems to have been set apart for African Americans. In other words, was the cemetery segregated?

Once you are home after interviewing relatives, especially older relatives, take a few minutes to record your thoughts. You may want to tape your impressions of the home your relative lives in and list any special artifacts that you may have been shown, especially if you were told they belonged to a forebear. One of my great-aunts, the last of ten children, kept something that belonged to each of her brothers and sisters, something the sibling in question cherished. She took great pride in taking these items out of special drawers from time to time and showing them to me. In the course of showing her treasures, she always added a little more to my information about that generation of my family.

Cameras

Among my most valued treasures are photographs of my forebears that have survived through the years. If you are permitted to take photographs of relatives, do so. (Do not overlook your own parents. Generations hence, your descendants will thank you for images of *their* forebears.) Do not limit your picture taking to people. Photograph old family homes, property that may have once been the site of family residences, churches, schools, workplaces, and train and bus depots that have meant something in your family's history.

You do not need an expensive camera for your work. In fact, some expensive cameras require more expertise than many of us have. Just get a simple, easy-to-use camera that will give you decent images. If you are taking pictures far from your home, take your film to a one-hour developer before leaving town. This way, you will know whether your pictures have turned out all right. If they have not, you can always retake them. The price of another roll of film is sure to be much less than that of a plane ticket or gas to return to the site to retake pictures.

A video camera, while not a must-have, is certainly a nice-to-have for your work. Even if you do not own a video camera, you may want to borrow or rent one for special occasions or special people. If you are lucky enough to have great-grandparents or grandparents who are living, a record of their images and voices will be priceless. Again, if you have access to a video camera, do not neglect filming your contemporaries. A hundred years from now, sights and sounds of their forebears will add meaning and depth to what your descendants know about you. (You will read more about preserving your family history in the last chapter of this book.)

USING THE INDIVIDUAL FAMILY WORKSHEETS

I've called the worksheet on pages 32–33 the Individual Family Worksheet. It is designed to go into your research notebook and permits you to record information about a single individual—perhaps a parent or a great-great-grandparent. It is a form I devised after months of transcribing notes taken on bits and pieces of paper while doing my own family history research. The worksheet is limited to a single page for easy use. When necessary, perhaps to record additional births or notes of interest, you can use the back of the page.

If you decide to use the Individual Family Worksheet, make as many copies of it as you like. You will find that the information you record on these sheets will provide some of the cross-references or verification that you will need throughout your search for your roots. For example, you can check the list of your maternal great-grandmother's children, recorded on her worksheet, against the list of your grandmother's siblings recorded on your grandmother's worksheet. If certain names do not match, you will know further research is required.

The worksheets should be placed in your research notebook according to surname. For example, if your paternal grandmother's maiden name was Lyle, include her individual worksheet with the Lyles even though her married name is Jones. On the Individual Family Worksheet for your paternal grandfather, include Lyle as part of his spouse's name—in this case, for instance, Martha Lyle Jones. Remember to include the full name of your ancestors whenever possible. For your female forebears, this means including their maiden names. As I mentioned earlier, knowing the maiden names of your female ancestors is vital.

To help you put the Individual Family Worksheets to good use, a sample is filled out for you. The completed worksheet applies to a woman named Mary Conover Anderson. Conover is her maiden name and consequently the surname I use for her. No such person exists. All the information about Mary Conover Anderson on the worksheet has been created as a guide to tell you what information to put in each space, and to give you some idea of what this information means.

Mary Conover Anderson lives at 810 Wood Street in Pittsburgh, Pennsylvania. She was born in Pittsburgh on the third of June in 1936. (You'll notice that on many old records, the day is written before the month. When recording dates for your own family, you may choose to put the day first, then the month, and finally the year, as many genealogists do.) Because Mary is still living, the date of her death and the burial site are not filled in. If you believe Mary to be dead but are not sure, simply put a question mark in the space for the death date, indicating that further research is needed. You would also use a question mark in the space provided to show the burial site. When you learn the burial site, fill in its name and address.

In the section SIBLINGS, you will notice that all have the same surname, except the first, Annie Lee Simmons. This suggests that Mary's oldest sister, a half sister really, was the child of a previous marriage who may or may not have grown up with Mary. In some such instances, children of other marriages are raised by another relative. Annie Lee Simmons may be able to provide you with information about Mary's roots that neither Mary nor her other siblings are aware of. Also note that the list of siblings includes one who died in infancy; this infant's burial site may be the burial site of other family members.

The worksheet indicates that although Mary Conover was born in Pittsburgh, she attended elementary school in Lindale, Georgia. Yet she attended junior and senior high school in Pittsburgh. Did her family move from Pittsburgh to Lindale and back to Pittsburgh again, or was Mary sent away from her family for a time? A check with the school Mary attended in Lindale may help answer this question. While Mary was in Lindale, she attended St. Paul's African Methodist Episcopal (AME) church. Was this a family church? Are important records available at the church or in the cemetery the church uses?

Mary's mother was born in Lindale, Georgia, where Mary attended elementary school. Did Mary's other siblings also attend school in Lindale? Did Mary live with one of her Jackson relatives while attending elementary school? Is Lindale, Georgia, a home place for the Jacksons, Mary's mother's family? Mary's father was born in Rome, Georgia. Is Rome a home place for the Conover family?

When did Mary's parents leave the South? We know Mary's mother must have left the South sometime between her own birth

INDIVIDUAL FAMILY WORKSHEET　　　　SURNAME:_____

NAME:_____

ADDRESS:_____

| Birth date | Place of birth | | Death date | Burial site |

Siblings:

1._____b._____d._____
2._____b._____d._____
3._____b._____d._____
4._____b._____d._____
5._____b._____d._____
6._____b._____d._____

Schools attended and locations:_____

_____

Churches attended and locations:_____

_____

Name of spouse:_____

| When married: | Where married: | By whom |

Children:

1._____b._____d._____Spouse_____
2._____b._____d._____Spouse_____
3._____b._____d._____Spouse_____
4._____b._____d._____Spouse_____
5. _____b._____d._____Spouse_____
6._____b._____d._____Spouse_____

Mother's Maiden Name and place and date of birth:_____

_____

Father's name and place and date of birth:_____

_____

INDIVIDUAL FAMILY WORKSHEET   SURNAME: Conover

NAME: Mary Conover Anderson
ADDRESS: 810 Wood St. Pittsburgh, Pa.

June 3, 1936	Pittsburgh, Pa.		
Birth date	Place of birth	Death date	Burial site

Siblings:

1. Annie Lee Simmons	b. May 2, 1930	d.	
2. Aubrey Dean Conover	b. April 18, 1932	d.	
3. Johnny James Conover	b. June 12, 1933	d. August 4, 1933	
4. Frances Ruth Conover	b. Jan. 10, 1938	d.	
5. Mary Louise Conover	b. Feb. 11, 1940	d.	
6.	b.	d.	

Schools attended and locations: Reed Elem., Lindale, Ga; Wilson JHS,
Pittsburgh, Pa.; Edison HS, Pittsburgh, Pa.

Churches attended and locations: Bethel AME, Pittsburgh, Pa.
St. Paul's AME, Lindale, Ga.

Name of spouse: Herbert Anderson

March 25, 1961	Bethel AME, Pittsburgh	Rev. Richard Wallace
When married:	Where married:	By whom

Children:

1. Herbert Anderson	b. Jan. 23, 1963	d.	Spouse	Lisa Wright
2. Dorothy Ann Anderson	b. March 4, 1965	d.	Spouse	
3. Martha Jean Anderson	b. June 5, 1966	d.	Spouse	Henry Butler
4. Paul Lee Anderson	b. Feb 7, 1968	d.	Spouse	
5.	b.	d.	Spouse	
6.	b.	d.	Spouse	

Mother's Maiden Name and place and date of birth: Annie Lee Jackson
Lindale, Ga. August 5, 1912

Father's name and place and date of birth: Harold Conover
Rome, Ga., February 6, 1907

in 1912 and Mary's birth in 1936, because Mary was born in Pittsburgh. We do not know if Mary's mother traveled directly from Lindale to Pittsburgh, however. Nor do we know when or even if Mary's father moved from Rome, Georgia, to Pittsburgh.

Since Mary is alive, she can provide firsthand (primary source) evidence about some of the time her father may have spent in Pittsburgh. She may also have letters written by her parents to their own parents or friends that may corroborate his residence in Pittsburgh. By checking the birthplaces of Mary's siblings, you may get closer to the time her mother arrived in Pittsburgh. If, for example, Annie Lee Simmons, the first child, was born in Pittsburgh, you will know that Mary's mother arrived in that city by at least 1930, when she was just eighteen years old. Did this eighteen-year-old undertake her journey from the South to Pittsburgh on her own, or was she accompanied by parents or other relatives? Was she being sent to Pittsburgh to live with other relatives?

By now, you've gotten the general picture and can see the wealth of information an Individual Family Worksheet can provide. If you are using this information on Mary Conover Anderson to trace your roots, you have three key cities that may hold important family information: Pittsburgh, Pennsylvania; Rome, Georgia; and Lindale, Georgia. As you complete other worksheets, opportunities to discover new or corroborating information will present themselves.

MAKING YOUR OWN GENEALOGICAL CHARTS

In the process of keeping track of the information you find, you will want to understand the relationships among various ancestors. The easiest way to do this is with genealogical charts. I have a decided preference for the charts used in many history books that trace the genealogy of royal families. I first became acquainted with them as a student, while trying to make sense of all those Tudors and Hapsburgs. When they were filled in, I found the charts clear and easy to read. As a consequence, I decided to use this history-book-type chart to keep track of various generations of my African-American family. A basic chart that covers two generations looks like this:

The chart can be developed in tiers, each showing a different generation. By layering the tiers, just as you layer tiers of a cake, you can always tell who your forebears were and when they lived. Let's see how it would work with your own family. All you need to begin is your mother's name, your father's name, and the names of your brothers and sisters. Even if you know only one parent's name, you can still begin your chart. The chart below shows two generations of a given family. Your chart will have more or fewer vertical lines, depending on the number of children your parents have.

In our example, your father was born in 1932 and died in 1982. If you did not know when your father died, you would put a question mark after his birth date—for example, "1932-?" According to the information on the chart, your mother was born in 1936 and is still living. The *m.* simply stands for the word *married*. When your parents' names are filled in, the line might read "Harold Wright m. Linda Johnson."

Your father (1932–1982) m. your mother (1936–)

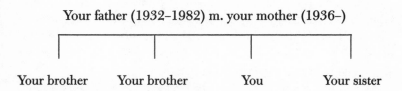

Your brother   Your brother   You   Your sister

In this example, your parents had four children. Now fill in their names, birth dates, and, if applicable, death dates. Can you see how the chart's simplicity makes it easy to read and easy to understand? When your schedule permits, make several of these two-generation charts and fill them in as your research permits.

Now let's assume that you want to show several generations of a family. Because the work is already done, I will show you as an example part of my own Thompson family genealogical chart. The chart on page 37 goes back to my paternal great-great-grandparents, Charles and Anastacia Anderson Thompson. You can see how the generations are tiered, or layered, one above another. To start with the earliest generation shown on the chart, you read from top to bottom. Seven generations of the Thompson family are shown on the chart, which represents just one branch of my family.

Now look at the chart again. What's missing? Despite a great many names and dates, the chart tells you virtually nothing about the Thompson family. Where did the family live? What work was the family engaged in? Were members of the Thompson family free people of color? Obviously they were not among those African Americans who changed their names after the Civil War. The family still has the name it had before that conflict began in 1861.

The information shown on the chart is gleaned from a wealth of family documents and oral histories—sources similar to those you will use to trace your roots. To give you an idea of the sources you will investigate, consider just one name on the chart, Edward Thompson, my great-grandfather. I found the date of his birth recorded in the family Bible. His death date was in a local newspaper, which also confirmed his birth date. His marriage to Ann Elizabeth Williams is supported by a marriage document and church records, both of which give the date and place of their marriage. Church records also testify to his membership in the Presbyterian Church. His children's birth records and death records verify his own. Family oral history, as told by three of his children, let me know that he was a logger by occupation.

As you can see from the top of the chart, my great-great-grandmother was named Anastacia Anderson. She represents an important branch of my family. The same can be said for my great-grandmother Ann Williams, my grandmother Maud Conover, and my mother, Agnes Richardson. Yet all the chart tells us about these women is that they married Thompson men and gave birth to Thompson children. What contributions did these women make to their own families and to the families they married into? As you learn more about individual members of your family—their interests, religious preferences, education, occupations, hobbies, and the towns they lived in—you will give meaning and substance to the information represented on your own genealogical charts.

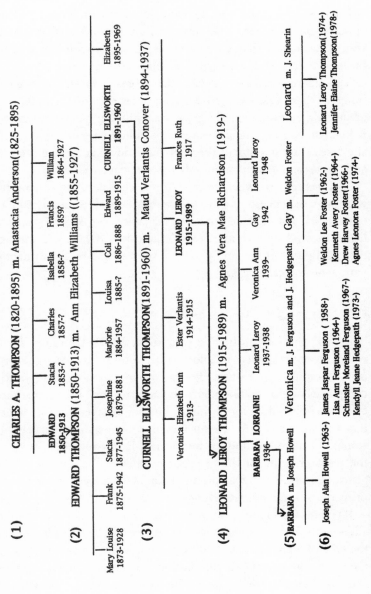

(1) CHARLES A. THOMPSON (1820-1895) m. Anastacia Anderson(1825-1895)

EDWARD 1850-1913 | Stacia 1853-? | Charles 1857-? | Isabella 1858-? | Francis 1859? | William 1864-1927

(2) EDWARD THOMPSON (1850-1913) m. Ann Elizabeth Williams ((1855-1927)

Mary Louise 1873-1928 | Frank 1875-1942 | Stacia 1877-1945 | Josephine 1879-1881 | Marjorie 1884-1957 | Louisa 1885-? | Coli 1886-1888 | Edward 1889-1915 | CURNELL ELLSWORTH 1891-1960 | Elizabeth 1895-1969

(3) CURNELL ELLSWORTH THOMPSON(1891-1960) m. Maud Verlantis Conover (1894-1937)

Veronica Elizabeth Ann 1913- | Ester Verlantis 1914-1915 | LEONARD LEROY 1915-1989 | Frances Ruth 1917

(4) LEONARD LEROY THOMPSON (1915-1989) m. Agnes Vera Mae Richardson (1919-)

BARBARA LORRAINE 1936- | Leonard Leroy 1937-1938 | Veronica Ann 1939- | Gay 1942 | Leonard Leroy 1948

(5) BARBARA m. Joseph Howell | Veronica m. J. Ferguson and J. Hedgepath | Gay m. Weldon Foster | Leonard m. J. Shearin

(6) Joseph Alan Howell (1963-) | James Jaspar Ferguson (1958-) Lisa Ann Ferguson (1964-) Schussler Moreland Ferguson (1967-) Kendyll Jeane Hedgepath (1973-) | Weldon Lee Foster (1962-) Kenneth Avery Foster (1964-) Drew Harvey Foster(1966-) Agnes Leonora Foster (1974-) | Leonard Leroy Thompson(1974-) Jennifer Elaine Thompson(1978-)

The numbers on the chart above show the relationship to Joseph Alan Howell, born in 1963: (1) great, great, great grandfather; (2) great, great grandfather; (3) great grandfather; (4) grandfather; (5) mother

Charles Thompson and his wife, Anastacia Anderson, did not appear from nowhere. They also had forebears. When you make your genealogical charts, be aware of the next higher tier and the one above that. And be aware of parallel tiers—tiers that let you put several different cakes on the table that represents your entire family. Some of these cakes will have common layers. For example, your great-great-grandmother shares layers with your great-great-grandfather. Although the family she was born into goes on without her, she takes from it some of the characteristics that are unique to it and passes some of them on to her descendants.

As I mentioned earlier, you can't research everything at once, but with time, patience, and good luck you will be able complete much of the work that must be done to trace your roots back to your earliest African-American ancestors. This trip may take you through the generations of the family that are represented by the women in your genealogical charts.

Considering Computers

The work involved in tracing your roots can be daunting. There will be countless pieces of information to find, sort through, organize, manipulate, store, and retrieve. You may wonder if you need a computer to help you find your way back to your earliest ancestors. Computers can do a lot of things, but one has yet to be designed that will go to a courthouse for you, or look for a particular tombstone in a burial ground, or interview a family member. In short, the research work of the genealogist must still be done by that genealogist. Still, using a computer can make some of your tasks—primarily storing and retrieving data—easier.

If you decide to buy a computer, make sure you have uses for it in addition to your genealogical activities. It would be difficult to justify the cost of equipment and software simply for genealogical work. Once you have justified purchasing a computer, however, most experts advise that you first select the computer software that does the task or tasks you want to do. This means you must give some thought to how you will use a computer. Once you have done so, you can select the computer that will run the software you plan to use.

I did not use a computer for genealogical research until I was ready to compile the research I had done into a history that I could share with my family. During my normal research activities, I found that the Individual Family Worksheets I used provided all the organization I needed. Because the information on these sheets was easy to access, I saw no need to recopy it simply to have it in a computer file. Still, you may feel that nothing in life is complete if it can't be connected in some way to a computer. If so, read on.

Word-Processing Software

If you want to stay with the plain and simple, or if you just want to start slowly, the word-processing software you choose for your other computer work will also help you with your genealogical work. You can get a demonstration of various word-processing software packages in virtually every major computer store. All these packages will permit you to store and retrieve data. Thus, if you organize your files well, you will always be able to find the information you have stored. A word-processing program will also permit you to copy and move blocks of text or charts from one place to another. This will be especially helpful when you find family connections that you did not know existed. For genealogical activities, it makes sense to choose a software program that also gives you enough graphic capabilities to make simple charts and graphs.

Once you have selected a word-processing program, you will discover that routine tasks become remarkably easier. For example, you can draft and store the letters you write to relatives or to personnel at archival centers and research facilities. With a few simple keystrokes you can change the names, addresses, or specific parts of a letter without having to rewrite it. When you're writing to request copies of vital statistics, for instance, you will only need to change the date and inside address. Moreover, because you can store each of the letters you write for follow-up or reference, you will have an easily accessible correspondence file.

Genealogical Software

Once you've decided to trace your roots, you may decide you want a software program that deals specifically with genealogy. New genealogy software is becoming available with ever-increasing frequency. These programs promise a great deal, and most deliver on their promises. Before buying one, however, be sure you really want and will use the features available.

Most genealogy software programs enable you to construct family trees, generate a variety of charts, and create family databases that will help you keep track of vital statistics. Some offer connections to Internet sites. Others provide historical data that may be useful and tutorials that can help you understand basic genealogical resources. You should know, however, that the historical databases offered in some programs—for example, the Social Security Death Index—are also available to those who do not choose to use the software. And some of the features available in genealogy programs (for example, identifying forebears through immigration and naturalization records, and drafting form query letters to appropriate authorities in European countries) will probably not be very helpful as you try to identify your African forebears.

Still, no one can quarrel with the graphics that genealogy software puts at your disposal. Most of the programs now available will permit you to create graphically beautiful family trees, design eye-catching pages of text, and even reproduce your data on disk or page. To create these family trees or charts or beautiful pages, however, you have to have some information to go on or in them. This information will come only from your research activities. When your research is done and you are ready to share its results, you may well want to publish your findings in some form. A genealogy software program may be of most use to you when you reach this point.

If you decide to purchase a genealogy software program, read the documentation (information on how the program works) carefully so that you know what you are buying. Then ask for a demonstration of the programs you think come closest to your goals.

Remember, genealogy software cannot do your research for you. In the final analysis, you will have to supply the basic information. But most programs now on the market will provide some guidance.

Online Access

You may decide that you need a computer so that you will have access to the databases that are available online; some can be very helpful in your genealogical research. Countless public documents, including census data and listings of archival resources and historical society holdings, are available on the Internet. Having access to this information can save time and help you reach your research goals.

Materials of particular interest to African Americans are also available online. For example, the Library of Congress has formatted its *African-American Odyssey* exhibition for presentation on the World Wide Web. The online exhibition is divided into nine categories: *Slavery; Free Blacks in the Antebellum Period; Antislavery Movements and the Rise of Sectional Controversy; The Civil War; Reconstruction and Its Aftermath; The Booker T. Washington Era; World War I and Postwar Society; The Depression, the New Deal and World War II;* and *The Civil Rights Era.*

In May 1998 the New York Public Library started its Digital Library Collections Web site. Readers can click on Digital Schomburg and gain access to a collection of more than fifty-six texts and five hundred images relating to nineteenth- and twentieth-century African-American history and culture. These materials are especially valuable in helping you understand the world in which your forebears lived. Many other online databases dealing specifically with concerns of African Americans are also available, and their number continues to grow.

You should know, however, that you do not need to buy a computer to gain access to the Internet and its databases. An increasing number of public libraries offer Internet access to patrons. Therefore, before you invest in a computer solely to gain access to databases, explore the resources available to you at your public library.

In many instances, you will be permitted to download information you believe will be helpful to you. Once the information is downloaded, you can make copies of it. In some public libraries, you will be permitted to make copies of a limited number of pages without cost. Thereafter, usually for a modest fee per page, you will be permitted to copy as much of the downloaded database as you think necessary. Don't get carried away with copying every database available, however; you can easily find yourself spending more money than you originally intended to make copies of information that is not very helpful. Sometimes making notes of what you see on the computer screen makes the most sense.

The number of local businesses dedicated to providing patrons with Internet access is also growing. You may find one in your local shopping mall or even in a computer store. For a fee, often determined by the time online and the copies made, you can search the Internet and download and copy data that may be helpful to you. If you are a college or university student, you may already have access to the Internet and the resources found there. You may also be connected to the Internet through your workplace. If so, you may wish to find out if personal use is permitted.

The Computer You Own

Perhaps you are a seasoned computer user. If so, you are probably well aware of how a computer can assist you in keeping track of your genealogy research data. You are also aware of your computer's limitations, including the one that limits your software selections to those your particular computer can handle. Your computer may not be able to run the newest, hottest genealogy program. Don't despair, though: You probably don't need the hottest or newest program to do the work you have in mind. Moreover, in this age of rapid technological developments, nothing stays hot or new for long. I have just one word of caution for the computer veteran: Genealogy is a people-intensive, not a computer-intensive, activity.

MOVING FORWARD

Now that you have thought about the work ahead of you and made a plan for organizing the information you find, you are ready to begin tracing your African-American roots. Like every other family, yours will have its saints and scoundrels, its workers and wastrels, its heroes and heels. And like every other person who undertakes this journey, you will find ancestors who make you proud and others who will make you want to hide your face. In the final analysis, however, you are the sum total of all of them—of all they were and all they achieved. No matter what you discover, one thing is certain: You will never regret deciding to begin the journey that takes you closer to the black and brown and red and yellow and white people who were and are part of your family. The journey will be exciting and rewarding. It may engage you for a lifetime.

3

Locating Family Documents

Every family has its documents. Some families treasure and preserve these records, keeping them in special places. Others toss family papers into a bottom drawer or tuck them away somewhere for safekeeping, only to forget where they've put them. Family documents—birth, baptismal, marriage, and death records; wills and deeds; letters and diaries—are essential to you if you are trying to trace your roots. For African Americans, these documents take on a special significance. Because so many of the records that pertain to our past were destroyed or lost, those a family has kept may be the only proof of an ancestor's existence. Family documents may contain the single piece of evidence available of a particular baptism, marriage, or burial. The records a family has saved over the years may include documents you need to trace your roots back to forebears who were free inhabitants of the United States at its beginnings. In short, finding, examining, and understanding the documents in your family's possession may lead you to your earliest African-American ancestors.

To be sure, birth, marriage, and death records; wills and deeds;

and a number of other comparable documents that pertain to your family may be found elsewhere—in courthouses or town halls, for example. There is no guarantee, however, that you will find what you need in a courthouse. An exploration of records there may fail to turn up proof of a birth or marriage that you know took place, especially if the event occurred before marriages or births were routinely registered. Further, many records stored in courthouses or town halls were destroyed by fire or flood. As a consequence, some of the documents that are still in family hands must be used to fill the gaps that exist in public records.

Certainly, public records will be important to you in your search for your African-American ancestors. No matter how many of these records were lost or destroyed, valuable information still exists in public places. When it is time to look outside your family for documents that will help you trace your roots, this book will guide you to the places most likely to house such records. For the moment, however, focus on locating those in your family's possession. Each one you can find stands to save you hours of research and perhaps considerable expense.

Rounding up existing family documents may be difficult. One relative may have a grandfather's baptismal record, and another his death certificate. Someone may have kept a deed to family property, while someone else may have a copy of an ancestor's will, disposing of that property. Sometimes the search for family records will require you to sort through boxes of memorabilia that include such mundane things as souvenirs from a seaside vacation taken decades ago. Do not toss out or disregard those souvenirs without a little investigation; they may not be as inconsequential as they seem. Perhaps some relative chose this particular vacation spot because your family once lived there. If this is the case, the place may hold information that will take you closer to your African-American forebears.

Begin your search for family documents in your own home. When you have exhausted all the possibilities there, plan to continue the search when you meet with relatives to discuss what they know about your family's history. Some of them are sure to have records that hold important keys to your past.

BIRTH RECORDS

As recently as 1910, only ten states in the United States required registrations of births. By 1925 that number had grown to thirty-three. It was not until 1933, however, that all the states in the U.S. (forty-eight at the time) routinely required birth registration. Despite the requirement, maintenance of birth records has not always been as conscientiously done as we would hope. Often, when proof of birth date or -place was needed, an older sibling or a parent simply appeared before the appropriate magistrate, testified under oath to the birth of the person in question, and a birth document, sometimes in the form of a delayed birth certificate, was issued. (You will read more about such documents in chapter 5.)

When collecting birth records, a good place to begin is with your own and your parents'. These birth records, sometimes in certificate form, will list the parents of the newborn, the time and place of birth, and the attending physician. Collecting documents relating to your own birth may seem unnecessary; after all, you know who your parents are and when and where you were born. Generations from now, however, this information will be of value to your descendants.

Your parents' birth records will provide important information beyond the time and place of their births. Your mother's birth record, for example, will name her parents (your grandparents). It is likely that, at the time of her birth, these grandparents were living in the town your mother was born in. This town, which will be named in her birth record, may be a home place for your family. Locating birth records for even one of your four grandparents may enable you to discover where two of your great-grandparents were living when that grandparent was born. As you know, where things happened is important to your search for your African-American ancestors. Birth records can answer some of these where questions. The towns, counties, and states where parents, grandparents, and great-grandparents were born are often places where you will find other important family information.

How do you go about finding the birth records your family has kept? Sometimes you will find birth information stored with school records, since proof of age was often required for school enrollment. At other times birth records are kept with marriage records, especially if either the bride or groom needed proof that she or he was old enough to marry without parental consent. Perhaps you will find birth records exactly where they should be: in a nice, appropriately labeled file folder.

Be careful not to let your expectations of what a document should look like cause you to overlook the very document you are searching for. While you may be used to seeing birth records in certificate form, such was not always the case. In the late nineteenth and early twentieth centuries, it was not unusual for the doctor who delivered a child to simply write on a piece of paper that a baby boy or girl was born to a given set of parents on a given day in a given year. Obviously, everyone whose business it was to know knew to whom this piece of paper referred. At least then. In many cases, especially when home births were customary, no *official* birth document exists. However, these home births may have been recorded in a family Bible. In the absence of other evidence, Bible records have often been accepted as proof of an event.

Bibles are indeed good places to look for birth information. In fact, many editions of family Bibles contain special pages to record vital statistics: births, marriages, deaths. When you are using Bible records, certain cautions apply. Notice when the Bible was printed. For example, if it was printed in 1860, and all the family information it contains is *later* than 1860, you can be fairly sure that this information (for example, a birth date) was recorded when it occurred. If the Bible was printed in 1900, however, and includes information going back to 1860, it is safe to assume that information about events that occurred before 1900 was based on someone's memory. If possible, you will want to find some corroboration of these memories.

My paternal grandmother was a Conover. I found a great deal of information pertaining to the births of my Conover forebears in the Conover family Bible, once owned by my great-great-great-grandparents John and Hannah Oakes Conover. The Conover family Bible was printed in 1841. Under BIRTHS, someone wrote that John Conover was born in January 1817 and Hannah Oakes was born on December 25, 1828. Since these births predate the time when the Bible was printed, I know they were recorded from memory. The birth date of the first child born to John and Hannah is recorded as February 20, 1848, seven years after the Bible itself was printed. This is a good indication that this birth—and the ten that follow—were recorded when they occurred. It is interesting to note that the dates for the births of the Conover children appear to have been written in the same hand that recorded John's and Hannah's birth dates. Therefore, it seems fairly safe to assume that either John or Hannah was the record keeper and, as such, more than qualified to record his or her own birth date and that of his or her spouse.

You may also find birth information in any military records your family has held on to. My great-great-uncle William Thompson enlisted in the Tenth U.S. Cavalry, one of two all-African-American cavalry units, in 1888, at age twenty-four. The Thompson family Bible records his birth date as July 12, 1864. His military record confirms the Bible record. My great-uncle William Holmes, a World War I veteran, was discharged from the U.S. Army on August 30, 1919, after two years of service. His discharge papers state that he enlisted at age twenty-nine. From this information, I know he was born in 1886.

Treat any original birth records you find with care. When copying the information they contain onto Individual Family Worksheets, lay them on a flat, clean surface so that you keep handling and soiling to a minimum. Do not carry original birth records around with you or paste them in your research notebook. Do not even fold them. Set aside a safe place to keep these and other valuable documents.

MARRIAGE RECORDS

One of my most cherished documents is my great-grandparents' wedding certificate. However fine it looked when they received it, today it is simply a deteriorating piece of paper that someone at some time pasted on a piece of cardboard. Still, I can read most of what it says: "Edward Thompson and Ann Williams were married on August 23, 1872 in the First Presbyterian Church in Whippany, New Jersey." Because of the sentimental value attached to marriage records, when they exist, they are likely to have a special place among family treasures. Perhaps you will find that one or two wedding certificates have been framed. When picture frames were hard to come by, a single frame was sometimes made to do double duty: Do not be surprised to find a wedding certificate under a family photograph for instance. It may be worth your while to undo the frames that hold old photographs to see if anything is concealed underneath.

National collection of statistics on marriages in the United States were made for various years from 1867 to 1940 and for each year since 1944. Like birth registrations, marriage registrations in the early years of their existence were not always kept carefully or routinely. When they can be located, you will find that Certificates and Records of Marriage provide much more information than the names of the couple being married. The document will identify the marriage site; this alone may be an important link to your past that you will find in no other place. A Certificate and Record of Marriage may also list the age, occupation, birthplace, and parents of both bride and groom. The officiating clergyman and his affiliation may be cited, too. Starting in the 1920s, information about the license to marry and the licensing official has often been provided. You will want to study each marriage record carefully, taking note of all the information it contains.

You are most likely to have access to your parents' or grandparents' wedding certificate. If your mother and grandmother are like most, however, you will find them unwilling to part with these cherished documents. You will probably be permitted to record the information they contain on the Individual Family Worksheets in your research notebook. You may even be permitted to borrow marriage certificates long enough to have copies made. Remember to handle original marriage records with the care valuable family documents deserve.

Once again, the family Bible is a good place to look for information about family marriages. (All the precautions I mentioned above about using Bible records apply here.) While the Conover family Bible listed only the marriage of my great-great-great-grandparents in 1847, the Thompson family Bible contained marriage information about many of my Thompson and Conover relatives. For example:

> Mr. and Mrs. Chester Edwards were married at Belleville on May 19, 1923.
> Mr. and Mrs. John Stevens were married at Belleville on May 19, 1923.

You might be intrigued by the matching dates of these marriages. Of course, it helps if you know that Mrs. Chester Edwards and Mrs. John Stevens were my paternal grandmother's sisters—Gladys and Mary Conover. Moreover, both lived at home with their parents in Belleville, New Jersey, and were married there.

Newspaper clippings announcing the marriage of an ancestor may be included among family papers. Depending on the paper, there may be just a line or two, or there may be a full-blown description of the nuptials. Always check the dateline. To learn that "Mr. and Mrs. Joseph Lee were married yesterday" when you have no idea when yesterday was will be of little help. Still, if you have the clipping and the name of newspaper, you may be able to find the date by checking the weddings listed in the newspaper index. You may also find an old church bulletin for a service that occurred on the same day that a family wedding took place. If so, the bulletin will help you pinpoint the day and year of the wedding. Even if the bulletin you find is not connected with a marriage, it may identify a church that has family significance. Hold on to it.

Do not be discouraged if you are unable to find Certificates and Records of Marriage among your family papers. As you continue your research, you may find that relatives have been entrusted with these records for safekeeping or simply latched on to them when a sibling died. If neither is the case, however, you may be able to find marriage information among public records. These will be discussed in chapter 5.

DEATH RECORDS

There is something about dying that encourages the saving of information. You will probably find among your family papers at least a few of the programs that were handed out at burial services. These programs will include some information about the deceased, identify those who officiated at the burial service in question, and name the place of internment. The member(s) of the clergy who officiated at family funeral services and the cemeteries these family members were buried in may hold important keys to your past. It is not unusual for funeral programs to contain a photograph of the deceased. This photograph may help you attach a name to another photograph you previously could not identify.

Among your family records you are also likely to find death notices that were published in the local paper. The notice of my grandmother's death in 1937 was the first one that I found published in an obituary column. Before then, death notices relating to my family were always among the paper's news items. I still do not know if the paper charged for obituaries and my family did not or could not pay, or if there was some other reason for this odd placement of notices relating to their deaths. Still, I must admit that finding my great-great-great-grandmother's death notice in the news items near the front of the local paper gave her death a certain prominence, at least from my late-twentieth-century point of view. The notice, which appeared on May 9, 1890, was direct and to the point:

While Mrs. John Conover, a respectable colored woman, was washing on Monday at the residence of George Reve, she dropped dead from heart disease. Coroner Hazen viewed the body and granted a burial permit without an investigation.

When you are ready to look for published death notices for your forebears, it still makes sense to check obituary columns. However, do not limit your search to those columns.

As you have come to expect by now, the family Bible will most likely include some death information. The sooner it was recorded, however, the more likely it is to need some clarification. The first entry under DEATHS in one of the Thompson family Bibles reads: "Dear Mother died on Feb. 12, 1912 at 4:20 A.M." I learned that this entry was written by my grandmother on the death of her own mother. The death had to have been traumatic for my grandmother, who was eighteen at the time. Her mother was just thirty-eight when she died.

Perhaps you will find copies of Certificates and Records of Death among your family documents. Your family may have needed them to settle estates, collect on insurance policies, satisfy creditors, or some other reason. I feel lucky to have a copy of the Certificate and Record of Death for my great-great-grandmother Elsy Elizabeth Conover Deree. The document lists her parents. If I hadn't already known who they were, this information would have been invaluable. In addition to naming her parents, the Certificate and Record of Death gives her age to the day, tells where she was born, where her parents were born (information that was new to me), what she died of, and where and when she was buried.

This information ought to satisfy anyone. Right? Well, perhaps not. When looking at the information provided on Certificates and Records of Death, it is important to remember that the person best able to provide the information requested is the deceased. Since that is not possible, you must evaluate the reliability of the person who did provide the information. In this case, the informant was George S. Deree. The document does not specify his relationship to the deceased or his age. He could have been my great-great-grandmother's husband, her son, a brother-in-law, or some wayfaring stranger of the same surname. Just as important, there is no way of knowing if Mr. Deree had any reason to conceal information from public officials.

Happily, other research verified the information on the Certificate and Record of Death and proved George S. Deree to be as reliable as the *Farmer's Almanac* though no more information was given about his relationship to the deceased. Still, it is always a good policy to verify the facts you find in official records. For example, my great-aunt Elizabeth provided the information contained on her sister Marjorie's Certificate and Record of Death. She reported that her sister had never been married. Yet I have in my possession my great-aunt Marge's marriage certificate. This marriage is further corroborated by the records of the First Presbyterian Church in Whippany.

Even if the information you find in death records requires verification, copy it onto your Individual Family Worksheets. Simply put a question mark or the word *verify* in parentheses after the information you want to check. And remember, the information a Certificate and Record of Death contains may well be correct. You simply want to do everything you can to assure that the data you collect and record is as accurate as possible. Sometimes the best we can do is come close to the truth. Considering all the events that have taken place in your family since your forebears came to these shores—not to mention the number of family members who have shaped these events—"close" is not always a bad place to be.

WILLS

Family wills let you know something about the assets your forebears were able to acquire during their lifetimes and, perhaps even more important, those to whom they chose to leave their worldly goods. Many of my forebears died intestate—that is, without leaving a will. Whatever possessions they had probably passed on to their next of kin. Leaving a will, however, is no guarantee that squabbles about possessions will not occur.

The oldest will in my possession is that of my great-great-uncle

William Thompson, who returned to Whippany after being mustered out of the Tenth U.S. Cavalry in 1893. His will is dated November 22, 1927. He died less than one month later, on December 18, 1927. His estate consisted of an "automobile truck" and a house. Never having married, William had neither wife nor child to consider when making his will. He chose to favor his brother Edward's oldest son; his sister-in-law, Edward's wife; and his niece, Edward's daughter. His choice of beneficiaries caused conflict that lasted well into the 1950s.

If you find wills among your family papers, note the city, county, and state where they were executed. This location may be a place of significance in your family's history. Also pay attention to the names of those who witnessed the signing of each will. Although these witnesses may not be related to the testators (those making the wills), knowing something about them may lead you to information that can be of value in finding your earliest African-American ancestors. If you do not find wills among your family records but you know that your forebears made them, you may find copies among public records in the county or counties in which the wills were executed.

DEEDS

If deeds are included among your family's possessions, they are not likely to be misplaced. Deeds represent property ownership and are usually accorded the respect they deserve. In your search through family documents you may find deeds referring to property that once belonged to your family but has since been sold. Do not consider these documents useless. Any property your family owned takes you to a state, county, and town that may hold other important family information. Moreover, by identifying the grantee (buyer), deeds provide the name of one or more of your property-owning forebears. Deeds also identify the grantor, the person(s) who sold the property in question. The seller may also be a forebear, since it was not unusual for family members to deed or sell part of their property to family members.

Older deeds are attractive documents and, when framed, often make nice pieces of artwork. As a consequence, you may find a family deed hanging on a relative's wall. It is not unusual for some relatives, especially older ones, to believe that the possession of a deed means possession of the land to which the deed refers, even if that land was sold long ago. You may find that they are determined never to let the deeds they hold out of their possession, even for the few moments it would take you to make copies of them. Don't despair. A deed usually contains a notation about the deed book in which it is recorded. If the records have not been damaged or destroyed, you can go to the courthouse, request the appropriate deed book, and obtain copies of the deed in question.

Do not expect to get a nice typewritten copy of the deed or even a copy as easy to read as the printed form hanging on your relative's wall. If the deed is old, it is likely to be handwritten, and copying it may well challenge your best deciphering skills. Still, you will have a copy of a family deed. This deed may provide clues about your family that you will find nowhere else. If the task of deciphering a deed seems too daunting, remember that you do not have to do it all at once. Remember also that over time you can become quite expert in reading old documents. It is a skill that will serve you well.

The oldest deed I have in my possession is dated March 31, 1868, and represents property my great-great-grandparents acquired in Whippany, New Jersey. The deed gives the exact location of the property in question and names the owners of the adjoining properties. It also names the grantor and grantee of the property. Where is this deed? Hanging on my living room wall in a very attractive frame.

LETTERS

Letters written from one family member to another can be more valuable than they seem at first glance. Some, by informing relatives of safe arrival in a new city or town, may document a family's migration. Other letters may recount day-to-day activities, describe employment opportunities, or report significant family events.

Unfortunately, most letters written to relatives do not contain surnames; they often begin, "Dear Sister" or "Dear Uncle Pomp." Still,
note any place-names or family names the letters contain.

If you are lucky, you will find some letters in their original
envelopes, which will provide the full name and address of the
person to whom the letter was sent. Even if the envelope does not
contain a return address, if it was sent through the mails it will
include a postmark, which will indicate not only the origin of the
letter but also when it was mailed. If the letter was delivered by
hand, however, the envelope may contain only a given name and, as
a consequence, be of little help in identifying the recipient. Still,
during your conversations with family members, someone is sure
to know the person to whom the letter was sent and something
about the person who wrote it.

In addition to letters from relatives, you may find other correspondence that will help you learn more about your family and corroborate information you have found elsewhere. This may include
letters from landlords that, while concerning rent increases, also
verify addresses; letters from schools calling attention to registration dates or truancies, written on stationery that documents school
names and locations; letters from a town official announcing tax
adjustments, thereby signifying property ownership; or letters inviting the recipient to church functions, confirming other information
about church membership.

Shoe boxes and cardboard cartons seem to be favorite repositories for correspondence. You may find an interesting collection of
letters stored away in your attic or at the back of a closet. Do not
overlook it. Until you are able to prove otherwise, consider all written documents valuable. Each may be some small piece of the
puzzle that is, at the moment, your family's past.

Diaries

If your search through family documents turns up an old diary,
count yourself very lucky. The diary may have belonged to a grandmother who describes her life or work or community. It may note

births, baptisms, marriages, and deaths of family members, the departure of a beloved uncle for the North or the West, and even favorite foods or clothes. All of this information will help you anchor at least one branch of your family in a given time and place. The diary can also provide names and events you may find nowhere else. In turn, these names and events may help lead you to earlier generations and closer to your roots. Equally important, the information contained in a diary is sure to offer glimpses into the life of an African-American ancestor. Only talking with this ancestor face to face could be more revealing.

PHOTOGRAPHS

In the last century and a half most families, regardless of their economic circumstances, seem to have found some way to have their images recorded. Daguerreotypes, tintypes, or old black-and-white photographs give form and substance to the names on your genealogical charts. You can be sure that the photographs you find in your own home or in the homes of relatives are images of people loved and cherished. Sometimes a name and date will be written on the back of the photo. As with letters, surnames may not be included. Still, someone in your family is likely to know the person photographed. In fact, other family members may have photographs taken at the same time that show not only the person in your photo but still more family members as well. The name and address of a photographic studio may be recorded somewhere on the photograph. Make special note of this information, which may provide another town to add to your list of places to search for information about your family.

Treat the photographic images with care, giving special consideration to those that are in disrepair due to age, handling, or improper storage. If you find old photographs pasted in albums, do not try to remove them. Leave this task to a professional. When you can, have restored any special photographs you find that are deteriorating. If possible, make copies of old, interesting, or unusual photographs to take with you when you interview family members.

Sometimes old photographs awaken memories that can unlock important doors to the past.

MILITARY RECORDS

African Americans have fought and died in every war in which the United States has been involved. If members of your family served in the military, their military discharge papers are likely to have been kept in a safe place. You will most likely find them among your family's most important records—for example, records of birth or marriage or copies of wills and deeds. The safekeeping of military documents was much more than a matter of pride in having served the country. Most military men and women were entitled to pensions or other benefits, so anyone who served wanted to be able to document this service. Important information about age and residence as well as length and place of service can be gleaned from military records. If you are lucky enough to find military documents among your family's papers, treasure them.

OTHER FINDS

In your search for family documents, you may well uncover school yearbooks that contain photographs and other information about relatives; report cards that list the names and locations of schools; old books that have been inscribed with names of forebears; newspaper clippings that mention births, deaths, marriages, or other items of family interest; and programs from special events, perhaps a recital or other performance, that a relative took part in. Scrapbooks themselves can be repositories for a wealth of information. Most contain a variety of items that pertain to the life or activities of a given family or family member. As a consequence, they are especially helpful in identifying avenues of research you may not have otherwise thought of.

All of these items may play a part in helping you trace your roots. You do not have to know at this moment exactly how a yearbook or a particular photograph will help in your search for your earliest

African-American ancestors. Perhaps something as simple as an elementary school report card will identify a city or a person who will further your research. Perhaps a newspaper clipping about a family celebration lists relatives you knew nothing about—relatives who may have some of the documents you need to identify another branch of your family. Before long, using papers, documents, and mementos now in your family's possession, you will be able to start putting together pieces of the puzzle that is your family's past.

Now What?

You may be uncertain of what to do with all the documents you have collected in your home or from relatives. As I discussed in the last chapter, you should categorize the information, keeping all like documents—all records of marriage, for example—in one place. Once it is categorized, you will want to transfer all appropriate information to your Individual Family Worksheets (if you have not already done so). For example, if a family Bible notation says that a grandfather died on March 27, 1945, but a funeral program for his burial service gives his death date as May 27, 1942, you will want to include both dates on his Individual Family Worksheet, indicating the source of each and making a note to verify the actual date of his death. When you have transferred all appropriate information to the worksheets, file the documents, either as I discussed in chapter 2 or in the way you feel will make these materials easiest to use. If you have documents that do not lend themselves to being placed in a file folder, store them at the back of one of the file drawers in space you have provided for this purpose.

Now you are ready to search out other information that may be available to you within your family. Simply put, it's listening time.

4

Finding Family Talkers

Passing family history from one generation to another runs deep in the African tradition. On more summer nights than I can remember, free of the obligation of school the next day, I sat on the back porch with older relatives, swatting mosquitoes, sipping cool drinks, and listening as they shared their memories. When tales were especially exciting, I was permitted to stay up late into the night. I loved being part of a group of people who accorded some degree of importance to my presence among them. After all, my siblings and I were the audience on these occasions. Everyone else knew the tales.

Bits and pieces of some of the things we were told are still in our collective memories:

Remember how Granny Thompson could tell the name of everybody going past by the way he drove his horse and buggy?

Remember when Ol' Man Charlie Day took our pig as the last payment on this property?

We lived in the house that used to stand where the reservoir is now. The house didn't have any nails in it, only pegs. My father and his brothers took it apart, board by board, put it on his wagon, and brought it to Whippany. Took eight trips to get the job done.

He was the one who went out West to fight in them Indian Wars and brought home that crazy ol' Indian woman.

When Granny died they just laid her on the bed and covered her with a net so the flies wouldn't get at her. I was twelve years old when she died. We all took turns sitting with her until Ol' Man Hicks got her coffin built.

Conducting interviews with family members and friends is an important task when you are trying to trace your roots. The task takes on a special and undeniable significance for African Americans: Without the information contained in family oral histories, it is doubtful that any of us would be able to trace our roots back to the forebears who were taken from the African continent and brought to the shores of North America.

In order to *hear* what your relatives tell you, you must rid yourself of assumptions you may now have about African Americans. First and foremost, there is no *typical* African-American story. Not every African who was sold into slavery belonged to the same socioeconomic group. Not every African who landed on these shores came from the same part of Africa. Not every African American came to the British North American colonies as a slave. Some were indentured servants who acquired their freedom at the end of a specified time. In fact some of these, once freed, became slave "owners" themselves.

Not every African American lived south of the Mason-Dixon line. From the earliest period of this country's history, you could find African-American populations, both slave and free, in the Midatlantic and New England states. Not every African-American slave in the South picked cotton or harvested rice. Many were skilled and valued artisans. Some African Americans who were sold into slavery bought their freedom. Others were granted their freedom upon the death of their owners. Still others cast off slavery by escaping, sometimes traveling as far north as Canada. Despite rigid requirements designed to keep slaves illiterate, many learned to read and write in English, a language not their own. Some used these communication skills to champion the abolitionist cause. Others became eloquent spokespeople for freedom.

To repeat, then, there is no typical African-American story. This is one of the reasons your particular family's oral history is so important. It is in this history that you will find those things that make your family, your roots, special. It is in this history that you will find clues about your own family's experiences in this country. And it is in this history that you will find a place uniquely your own—a place that will give you an individual perspective on the African-American experience in the United States.

Of course, certain cautions apply when you are listening to family stories. Someone may believe a great-grandmother came from Africa when it was really a great-great-great-grandfather. Someone else may report that your family lived on a plantation in South Carolina when in fact the state was Georgia. Another relative may swear that a forebear was a tailor when he was really a cobbler surnamed Taylor. Still, don't dismiss any family stories without some investigation. There is usually an element of truth in each of them; your task will be to find this element. Just as important, some of your family's oral history will be completely reliable and will contain information that you will be able to verify.

PRIORITIZING INTERVIEW CANDIDATES

As I mentioned earlier, you will want to begin your family interviews with the oldest members of your family—those most likely to be overtaken by illness or death. Moreover, the information a younger relative possesses can sometimes be found in other places. The same may not be true of the information in the possession of an older relative, who may have been entrusted with important family documents generations old. Certainly it would be difficult for a young relative to compete with an older one when it comes to sharing memories that may have been part of your family's oral history for as long as anyone can remember.

It was my great-aunt Elizabeth, born in 1895, who guarded the deed for the property her grandparents (my paternal great-great-grandparents) acquired in 1868. Until her death in 1974, Aunt Liz was a faithful keeper of family treasures. Her greatest heartbreak was that the family trunk—one that contained documents dating back to her grandparents—was burned in 1954 in a fit of pique by a woman who had married into the family and who would no longer endure my great-aunt Marge's taunts: "That's a Thompson house. The Thompson trunk is in that house. You ain't got no right to be there." One hot August day that woman, my great-aunt Stacia's daughter-in-law, dragged the Thompson trunk from the attic, "set it on the front lawn, and just put a match to it." Fortunately, a few important family documents were not in the trunk that day. That woman happened to be living in that Thompson house by virtue of the will made by William Thompson, the Buffalo Soldier.

If you have a choice, visit the oldest relative who lives nearest your own home. If, however, you have great-grandparents or older grandparents who live some distance away from you, try to interview them at your earliest convenience and, if possible, spend a few days with them. You are likely to find other important family information in the area where they live. Therefore, a visit that lasts a few days may be well worth your while.

Do not be put off if an aging relative is living in a nursing-care facility. This facility may be located near a family home place and also warrant a few days' visit. And do not be afraid to trust an aging relative's family stories. Although many older people do not remember what happened yesterday, their memories of things that happened long ago are often crystal clear. Some knowledge of these events can be of enormous benefit to you as you trace your roots.

After you have visited with and interviewed your great-grandparents and grandparents, plan to interview older relatives who live nearby. These visits will help you hone your interview skills before you incur additional expense and invest more time traveling to visit with relatives who live some distance away. In fact, as your interviewing skills improve, you may wish to follow up on a few things with those great-grandparents you interviewed first.

PREPARING FOR THE INTERVIEW: ATTITUDE

An important part of preparing for an interview with a family member, especially an older one, is to think about how you will handle it. If things go badly the first time, you may not get a second chance, and it is most often these second and third interviews or chats that provide the most significant information. In fact, family members may spend much of the first interview sizing *you* up, trying to decide how much they can share safely. After all, you can never tell whose children are likely to put family business in the street.

How you ask for an interview is important. You certainly don't want to call an aunt and say, "Could I look through your papers to see if you have anything I could use for the family history I'm writing?" A typical response is: "I don't have any papers." Moreover, it won't matter what you say after that. Unless you have an influential relative who is expert at prying open doors that have been slammed shut, you have probably ended your chances for an interview with this particular aunt—and she may well report to other family members, "That child had the nerve to ask me if he could snoop through my stuff."

By the same token, most people are flattered to realize that others believe they have something of value to offer. It will be to your benefit to make plain the fact that you need help. Simply put, you do. If you see an older relative with some degree of regularity, perhaps at church or on family occasions, ask if you may visit at a convenient time. Say that you are trying to find out more about your family and you would like to talk with her about what you have learned so far. Do not make what you are asking her to do seem too difficult or like too much work.

If you must telephone a family member to arrange an interview, always identify yourself. I always say, "Aunt Biddie, this is Barbara calling, Buster's daughter." (My father was always called Buster by his aunts, and invoking his name has never failed to open their doors.) Of course, Great-Aunt Biddie (née Bridget Conover) prided herself on being difficult. No matter how often I talked with her on the telephone, her first response was always, "I don't know you children." That meant I had to butter her up, which I was always willing to do because she was one of our family keepers and had a wonderful memory.

When I visit relatives who have agreed to an interview, especially older ones, I dress! "My, don't you look nice today" has been the prelude to some wonderful family interviews. My older relatives, especially the women in our family, have never had very much tolerance for anyone "comin' in here looking like Ned in the First Reader." (Ned was the scruffy-looking one in elementary school readers. Everyone in my family knows Ned.)

Deciding What to Ask

It is important to think beforehand about the questions you will ask. Do not try to keep interview questions in your head. Write them on index cards or on something small. The sight of lots of sheets of paper or your bulging research notebook can be off-putting. You want the person you are interviewing to think you are concentrating on him and not your notes. And in truth you are, or should be.

You will, of course, tailor your questions to the person you are interviewing. And you will, of course, be sensitive to particular areas that may be painful for the interviewee to talk about. You may know that a relative's grandfather was lynched, but you certainly will not introduce that topic. If it is discussed at all, let your relative introduce it. If she does, you may pursue the conversation if you think it will add in any significant way to finding your roots. Information about the lynching, for example, may take you to a family home place and to family records located there.

Following are over two hundred of the kinds of questions you will want to ask relatives about your family's past. I have asked each of these questions more than once, although not all of them of a single family member. Each time I asked a given question, I received new information or information that confirmed things I had been told by others. Be assured that the following questions are intended only as a guide. Even if you decide to use them, it will not be necessary, or perhaps even possible, to ask all of them in a single interview or of every person you talk with. If you are lucky, however, and the interviewee is responsive, you may be able to get responses to questions that are important to you.

Do not plan to cover every topic in one sitting. This can be exhausting for you and for the person being interviewed. Once you have established contact and made a favorable impression, though, subsequent interviews can be arranged. In time, when you just need to check up on a fact or two, a relative may even be responsive to a telephone call, fax, or E-mail. Still, despite the variety of quick communication methods available today, nothing takes the place of a good chat. Unexpected and important information is not likely to be forthcoming via fax.

Your own knowledge of your family will permit you to develop countless questions of your own—some of which may not be included among those listed below. The questions drawn from your own knowledge, understanding, and experience are the ones most likely to help you find your roots. Ask these questions. Be sure to ask only the questions that it makes sense to ask. If the person you are interviewing tells you he never attended school, there is no need to ask questions that apply to his school experiences. You might ask about the education of other members of the family, however, and, if it does not seem to be unpleasant, you may want to explore what the person you are interviewing did instead of going to school. If he is still living in the same house he was born in, you need not pursue how often he moved, but it may make sense to discuss migrations of other family members.

Most important, do not try to get too much information from a single question. Ask simple and distinct questions. Obviously, this process takes time. Your patience will pay off. In the main, be guided by the answers you receive to the questions you ask. Sometimes an unexpected response may take you to unexplored and exciting territory.

If the person you are interviewing seems to be wandering off in all directions, let her drift for a while. She may be remembering events or people you need to know about. If she seems to be tired of discussing family life or traditions, switch to another topic. You can always come back to the one you were discussing at another time. One other caution: Older relatives may well refer to African Americans as colored or Negro. Once in a great while they may use the word *black* when referring to relatives. (Sometimes they will *mean* black, quite literally.) Most will not use the term *African American*. Accept whatever terminology they use without attempting to correct them. More than this, make every effort to also *use* the terminology they use. There is no point in letting semantics slow down or stall an interview.

HOME PLACES

1. What is the first house you remember living in?
2. Do you remember when that was?
3. Is that house still standing?
4. What state was that house in?
5. Do you remember the name of the county you lived in?
6. What was the name of town you lived in?
7. Do you remember how many rooms were in the first house you remember living in?
8. What was your favorite room?
9. Do you remember what other rooms in that house looked like?
10. What did your house look like from the outside?
11. How many members of your family (your mother, father, sisters, and brothers) lived with you in that house?
12. Did other relatives live in the house with your family?
13. Who were they?
14. Did other relatives live nearby?
15. What was the biggest town nearest your house?

16. Did you go there often?

17. What do you remember about visiting that town?

18. Was a courthouse located there? A bank?

19. How long did you live in the first house you remember?

20. Do you know if your family owned the first house you remember?

21. Do you know the name of the person who did own the first house you lived in?

22. When did you move from the first house you remember?

23. Did all of your family move with you?

24. Where did you move to?

25. Do you remember why you moved?

26. Do you remember other houses you lived in?

27. Where were those houses located?

28. Do you remember the names of the counties or towns those houses were in?

29. Did anyone ever tell you about houses the family lived in before you were born?

30. Do you know the names of any family members who lived in these houses?

31. Do you remember hearing anything about where these houses were located?

32. Do you remember hearing anything about how the family came to live in any of these houses?

PERSONAL DATA

1. Where were you born?

2. When were you born?

3. How many sisters and brothers do you have?

4. What are their names?

5. Do you remember when each was born?

6. Are all your sisters and brothers still living?

7. Do you remember when [name] died?

8. What was your mother's maiden name?

9. Where was she born?

10. When was she born?

11. What was your father's full name?

12. Where was your father born?

13. When was he born?

MARRIAGE AND CHILDREN

1. When did you marry?

2. Whom did you marry?

3. Where did you marry?

4. Did either you or your spouse marry more than once?

5. How many children did you have?

6. What are the names and ages of those children?

7. Did all of those children result from your marriage to one person?

8. Are all those children still living?

9. Did any of your children suffer any unusual accident or disease?

10. Did you name any of your children for a relative or an ancestor?

11. How did you learn about that name of your ancestor(s)?

EDUCATION

1. When you were growing up, did you have a chance to go to school?

2. Do you remember the name of the first school you attended?

3. What state and town was the school located in?

4. How did you get to school?

5. How many grades were in the school?

6. Did white and black children go to school together?

7. Do you remember what your school looked like?

8. Do you remember what the school white children attended looked like?

9. What is the name of the first teacher you remember?

10. Do you remember some of the subjects you studied?

11. Do you still have any of your report cards or school papers?

12. How many years were you able to go to school?

13. Did your brothers and sisters also attend school?

14. Did your parents have a chance to go to school?

15. How many years did your father attend school? Your mother?

16. Was the high school you attended near your home?

17. In what state and town was your high school located?

18. How did you get there?

19. Did black and white students attend the same high school?

20. What did your high school look like?

21. What did the high school white students attended look like?

22. Do you think you received a good high school education?

23. When did you first think about going to college?

24. What state and town was your college located in?

25. Was the college student body integrated?

26. Was the college faculty integrated?

27. Who encouraged you to go to college?

28. In what year did you graduate from college?

29. Why did you decide to pursue an advanced degree?

30. Where did you do your graduate studies?

WORK

1. When you were a child, did you have chores to do?
2. What were they?
3. Were you paid for doing these chores?
4. As a child, were you able to earn pocket money?
5. How did you earn it?
6. When you were a child, did your mother work outside the home?
7. Do you remember whom she worked for?
8. What work did she do?
9. Did she work near home?
10. How did she get to work?
11. Did she come home from work each day or did she stay at her workplace most of the time?
12. When you were a child, did your father work outside the home?
13. Do you remember whom he worked for?
14. What work did he do?
15. Did he work near home?
16. How did he get to work?
17. Did he come home each day after work or did he stay at his workplace most of the time?
18. Do you know how much your parents earned for their work?
19. Did your family ever move to find work?
20. Where did you move to?
21. Did other family members help your parents find work in other places?
22. What work did they find?

23. Did you ever hear stories about any family members being slaves?

24. Did you ever hear anything about where those slaves first came from?

25. Did the family members who were slaves work on a plantation(s)?

26. Do you remember hearing the names of the people who owned the plantation(s)?

27. What state was the plantation(s) located in?

28. What county was the plantation(s) located in?

29. Do you remember hearing stories about family members who escaped from slavery?

30. Where did the family members who escaped from slavery go?

31. Do you remember ever hearing stories about family members who were sharecroppers?

32. Did you ever hear the names of the people they sharecropped for?

33. Do you know the state they sharecropped in?

34. Do you know the county they sharecropped in?

FAMILY LIFE

Gatherings, Storytelling, and Traditions

1. What family celebrations do you remember most?

2. What was memorable about them?

3. Did your family ever have large gatherings of relatives?

4. Who attended these gatherings?

5. When your family got together, did family members share stories with each other?

6. What are some of your favorite family stories?

7. Did any of these stories go back to a time before any of the people present were alive?

8. What is the oldest story that is still told in the family?

9. Do you remember any old stories that have to do with slavery?

10. Do you remember any old stories have to do with life in Africa?

11. Were you ever told stories about plantation life?

12. When you think of family gatherings, were most of the people present part of your father's family or part of your mother's family?

13. Did both families live in the same town?

14. Are there special family traditions that are carried on generation after generation?

15. Do you know how these traditions started?

Names and Name Changes

1. Did you ever hear of your father's family or your mother's family having a different last name?

2. What was that name(s)?

3. Did you ever hear stories about why either family changed its name?

4. Are there any stories in the family about African names?

5. Do you remember any of those African names?

Racial Differences

1. Are any members of your family white?

2. Did those white members of your family have the same or a different last name?

3. Do the white and black members of your family live in the same place or in different places?

4. In what state do the white family members live?

5. In what state do the black family members live?

6. In what county do the black family members live?

7. In what county do the white family members live?

8. Are any members of your family Native Americans (American Indians)?

9. Do the black members of your family and the Native American members of your family live in the same place or in different places?

10. Did white and Native American people become members of your family through marriage?

11. Do you know how long you have had white relatives?

12. Do you know how long you have had Native American relatives?

13. Do you and your white family members share a common ancestor?

14. Do you and your Native American family members share a common ancestor?

The Family Bible

1. Does your family keep a family Bible?

2. Does your family Bible contain information on births, marriages, and deaths in the family?

3. Were you the first to use your family Bible?

4. How long has the Bible been in your family?

5. Who was the first to use it?

6. What is the first piece of information written in your family Bible?

Family Documents

1. Do you have a copy of the record of your birth?

2. Do you have a copy of the record of your marriage?

3. Do you have copies of birth records for other members of your family?

4. Do you have copies of marriage records for other members of your family?

5. Do you have copies of death records for other members of your family?

6. Do you have any old papers that have been in the family for a very long time?

7. Have you ever seen any very old letters written by family members?

8. Who has these letters now?

9. Did any family members keep diaries or records of how they spent each day?

10. Do these records or diaries still exist?

11. Who has them?

12. Have you ever seen very old photographs of family members?

13. Does anyone in the family still have these photographs?

14. Do you have any manumission documents—freedom papers—that granted freedom from slavery to any family members?

15. Have you ever heard of anyone in the family having very old family documents?

Religious Affiliation and Family Burials

1. When you were a child, did you attend church?

2. What church did you attend?

3. Where is that church located?

4. Has your family always attended a church of the same denomination?

5. Have you ever heard old stories about the family attending a church where most of the worshipers were white?

6. Do you remember hearing where that church was located?

7. Do you remember hearing any family name connected with membership in that church?

8. Where are family members buried today?

9. Have they always been buried in this place?

10. Are there old family stories about other burial places?

11. Do you remember hearing anything about the location of these burial places?

Military Service

1. Did any family members serve in the Korean or Vietnam War?

2. Did any family members serve in the Second World War?

3. Have you heard of any family members serving in the First World War?

4. Have you ever heard of any family member serving in the Spanish-American War?

5. Have you ever heard of any family member serving in the Indian Wars?

6. What is the oldest story in the family about a family member having served in a war?

7. Did any family member fight for the Union (the North) during the Civil War?

8. Did any family member fight for the Confederacy (the South) during the Civil War?

9. Are there old family stories about a family member having fought in the Revolutionary War?

10. Did that family member fight in the Revolutionary War because he was taking the place of someone else?

11. Have you ever heard the name of the person he replaced in the Revolutionary War?

12. Have you ever heard of a family member receiving a government pension because of service in the military?

13. Do you have any photographs of a family member in uniform?

14. Do you have any discharge papers for a family member who served in the military?

15. Are there old family stories about a family member who was involved in an African tribal war?

WRITING DOWN OR RECORDING
WHAT YOU HEAR

Your interview with a relative begins the moment you ring the doorbell. No matter how anxious you are to get down to the nitty-gritty, you must take time to exchange pleasantries and accept something of what is offered to eat or drink, even if you do not want anything. I never arrive at an interview site empty handed. I usually take a few simple flowers to a woman, and small pie or other baked item to a man. On subsequent visits I try to take a copy of some information I have uncovered that might be of interest. Whenever it is given, the gift must be simple, lest it appear that you are trying to buy the information you are seeking.

Once the interview has started, I ask permission to write down some of the answers. I always have several sheets of eight-and-a-half- by eleven-inch paper—folded in quarters—in my purse or pocket. These folded sheets look like something I just happened to have handy, and tend to be acceptable. (I once had an eighty-year-old cousin ask me, "Is that the best paper you've got? I can give you something better than that to write on," whereupon he produced a very old, unused notebook. "You might as well keep that. I knew it would come in handy someday.") Be prepared to write down as much of what you hear as possible. The fact or date or comment that seems insignificant today may turn out to be important.

Always start with questions that evoke pleasant memories. I have found that questions dealing with childhood homes or family traditions usually get the interview off to a good start. Once the interview is well under way, it becomes easier to get to personal data without seeming to pry. I try not to interrupt someone who wanders off course. These excursions often provide information I might not have thought available.

Sometimes the person you are interviewing will refer to an event—for example, "The War"—and you won't be sure which war is in question. If it is World War II, the person you are interviewing will probably be able to provide the date, if you ask. But if the war in question is the Spanish-American War, your interviewee may not be able to give you an accurate date. He may know that a relative took the Freedom Train out of slavery but have no idea when the Underground Railroad was most active.

To make sense of some of the information you acquire during your interviews, you may need to know when certain events occurred. This knowledge can be important to an understanding of African-American history in general and to your family history in particular. For example, you may learn that a relative fought in the Indian Wars—but to find him in existing records, you need to know when these wars occurred. One of your forebears may be remembered for having been born the day slavery ended. Does this mean she was born on January 1, 1863, upon the enactment of the Emancipation Proclamation, or on December 6, 1865, when the Thirteenth Amendment to the U.S. Constitution was ratified? You can find much of the historical information you need in a basic chronology of African-American history. There are several to choose from. Although published almost twenty years ago, I have always found the *Chronological History of the Negro in America* by Peter Bergman helpful. (See the bibliography for more information on this and other history books.)

If you are lucky, you may be permitted to record interviews. As I mentioned earlier, have a small, battery-powered tape recorder available for this purpose. You may find, however, that information considered private or "family business" may be withheld if the interview is being taped. Such "family business" may include information that seems quite commonplace today—an illegitimate birth, a divorce, substance abuse. Still, some family members may feel obligated to keep the information in the family. If you sense that the tape recorder or even your note taking is impeding conversation, turn off the recorder or put down your pencil and listen. I've done this more than once, and more than once I've learned things about my forebears that opened doors I didn't know existed.

Once an interview is over, be sure to express your appreciation for the time and information you have been given, and be sure to ask if you may visit or call again. Once you are back at home, organize your notes as quickly as possible, especially if you have been forced to try to remember everything you were told. Transfer as much as you can to the appropriate Individual Family Worksheets. Make notes that will allow you to follow up with the family member you have just interviewed or with another family member. Telephone or write a note expressing thanks for the interview. And do keep in touch with the people you interview, even if you think you have exhausted the information they have to share. Your life will be enriched by contact with them. Moreover, relatives sometimes come through with important information months or even years after the initial interview. "I just found some old letters tucked away in a wooden box. Think they might be of any use to you?"

CONTACTING STRANGERS

There will come a time when your search for your roots will require you to contact relatives who are complete strangers. Perhaps more than one relative has told you of an aunt who knows family stories about slavery or has an old family Bible with birth and death records going back to the early 1800s. Someone with this kind of information warrants a visit—but how can you make sure you will be received? After all, this aunt doesn't know you from Adam. I believe that the best way to contact her is by letter. A letter gives her the kind of time and space a telephone call does not. Such time and space provide the opportunity for her to decide whether she wants to see you and, more important, whether she wants to share with you the information she has.

You may have to talk with several relatives to find out that she now lives in Detroit, has married for the third time, and consequently has a new surname. Once you have her name and address, write your letter. Below is an example of the kind of letter you may want to write. Of course, as with all examples in this book, be guided first by your own knowledge and understanding of your family and of what will work best in any given situation.

Dear Aunt Martha,

Aunt Lou said that you might be able to help me find out more about our family. She gave me a copy of a page from an old family Bible but I can't make out all the names and dates. I was hoping you would be able to help me.

I would love to visit you and to bring some of the information I have collected from other family members. I could get off from work any time next month. May I visit you then?

Please call me and let me know if I may come. My telephone number is (312) 555-4413. Be sure to reverse the charges. I look forward to hearing from you.

Sincerely,
Your grandniece Barbara (Buster's daughter)

Although many relatives may have information that can help you trace your roots, not all of them warrant a visit. When you are trying to establish contact with them, however, all should receive some kind of written communication from you. And all should receive from you some family information as one way of encouraging them to help you. Relatives are much more willing to help when they believe others are doing the same. The easiest gift to send a relative is part of the genealogy chart that applies to her branch of the family. I always ask her to add to the chart any names I may have omitted and return it to me—promising, of course, that I will send a corrected chart when it has been completed. Then I may say something like: "Aunt Lou told me that you have a copy of Great-Grandmother Conover's birth record. Would you be kind enough to make a copy of that record for me?" Do not be surprised when a relative sends you more than you ask for—perhaps a copy of a death certificate or will. Getting involved in collecting family history is often contagious.

After you have established contact with a relative, maintain this contact. Once or twice each year, I let those who have helped me know how things are going. I also try to share new information that may be of special interest. "I just found out that Great-Granny Thompson held quilting parties at her house every other Friday afternoon and that your grandmother Sadie attended. Do you know if anyone has any of those quilts?"

It is often possible to meet relatives who are strangers to you by attending as many family gatherings as possible. You may even want to host a few yourself. Such gatherings often turn up an odd cousin or two who may have access to some of the information you seek. Family gatherings are also good places to tap into family stories. Seeking and paying attention to family oral history is an ongoing activity. Someone will always have a new story to tell or a new twist to add to an old one. As you continue your research, you will be able to make sense of some family tales you may once have thought unimportant. You will also be able to add information to old stories that have been told for so long that some of the details have been lost.

As you travel back in time toward your roots, your appreciation for your family's oral history will grow. The words you hear will form paths that will lead you to more information, and perhaps in new directions. As you find your family's talkers, you will learn that the tools you need most are the abilities to *listen* and to *hear*. Many people listen to old family stories but they do not actually hear what is being said. When a relative tells you, "We don't know where that child came from," he may be telling you that you need to check on the parentage of a given forebear. If he says, "That's just the way we've always done it," he may be describing a family tradition that is generations old—a tradition that may have had its origins on another continent.

Because your family's oral tradition is so important, you will want to have it available for future reference. Keep a section titled ORAL HISTORY at the back of your research notebook. List there the names that keep cropping up—names that seem familiar to several family members, although no one is sure of their origin; descriptions of forebears who died long ago but maintain a place of importance in family history; occupations that may have been engaged in by your ancestors; names of rivers or towns or counties that seem to have some bearing on your family's sojourn in this country; strange-sounding names that may be African in origin.

As you continue your search for your roots, your family's oral history will contribute in no small measure to your success in finding your African-American forebears. Your search will not be easy, but without your family's oral history, it would be virtually impossible. This seems reason enough to value your family talkers. Listen to and hear all they have to say. Think about becoming one yourself. Griots (people who are charged with remembering and sharing the history of a particular tribe or village) are still in fashion.

5

Examining Town and County Records

Your examination of important documents still in your family's possession and conversations with family members about your common past has exposed you to ancestors who may have been unknown to you. You now have a few names to put on genealogy charts and some places and events to record on Individual Family Worskheets. You are beginning to see just how much information you have and how much more you must find. At the moment the names, dates, and places you do not know may seem to far outweigh the information you have gathered. While you may have verified a few dates that go back as far as 1900—a great-grandparent's birth, for example—you despair of ever tracing anyone or anything back to the 1800s. And if you cannot do this, how are you going to find your earliest African-American ancestors?

It should be encouraging to know you have just begun to scratch the surface of all the data that is available to help you in your search for your forebears. You may be able to locate some of this data in the towns and counties they lived in. The data, which includes birth, marriage, death, and tax records, as well as copies of wills and deeds, is usually in the keeping of a town or county clerk. Even if you have found some of these documents in your own home or in the possession of relatives, there are others you will need to examine. Be assured that the work you have done thus far will serve you well. Your familiarity with the form and content of various kinds of documents will expedite your review of those documents kept with other public records.

From this point on, your success in finding your earliest African-American ancestors will be directly linked to your ability to identify these ancestors by surname. Many African Americans face at least three distinct hurdles in finding these surnames. First, Africans who were transported to North America on slave ships were rarely permitted to keep their African names. If they were given a surname, it was usually the surname of the man or woman who bought them. More often, however, African-American slaves were known only by a given name, perhaps Caesar or Pompey or Sally. The second problem in finding a surname grew out of emancipation. Once freed from bondage, many former slaves took new names as one way of embracing freedom. Finally, in the 1960s and early 1970s, in a burst of newfound pride in blackness and all it represented, countless African Americans cast off the surnames that had identified their families for generations and took on names they believed more accurately represented their true ancestry. LeRoi Jones became Imamu Amiri Baraka; Lew Alcindor became Kareem Abdul-Jabbar; Malcolm Little became first Malcolm X and then Malcolm Shabazz. Today, African Americans continue to choose for themselves and for their children African- or Islamic-sounding names.

To be sure, African Americans are not the only Americans to have changed their surnames. Others, sometimes to avoid perceived prejudices against the ethnic group they belong to, changed their surnames to those they believed more acceptable to their neighbors and employers. Some found themselves with a new name simply because immigration officials could not spell foreign surnames. Most of those who changed their names or had these names

changed for them are well aware of the surnames their ancestors
bore for generations. Many African Americans, however, stripped of
their identity by slavery, have no idea of the names that originally
identified their African families.

FINDING THE RIGHT SURNAMES

At some point during your search for your earliest African-
American ancestors, you will focus on two key surnames: your
father's surname and your mother's maiden name. Perhaps one or
both of your parents took new surnames during the 1960s or early
1970s. To trace your roots back to earlier generations, you must
know the surnames your parents were given at birth. You can ask
your parents for the information, of course. You can also find these
surnames on their birth certificates. If birth records are not available
to you, and if your parents had their names legally changed, a
record of these changes will be on file in the county where they
were registered. The same will apply to your grandparents if they
are responsible for changing a family surname.

Once you identify the surnames your parents or grandparents
were given at birth, you will be able to use these names to trace
your family back to the ratification of the Thirteenth Amendment to
the U.S. Constitution, which occurred on December 6, 1865. It was
this amendment that officially ended slavery in this country. (The
Emancipation Proclamation, signed by President Abraham Lincoln
on January 1, 1863, freed only those slaves residing in states that
were in rebellion against the United States.)

When you have traced at least some of your forebears back to
1865, you will have to determine if your family has a history of slavery. As I mentioned above, the surname your ancestors used during
slavery may well have been the surname of a slave owner. Compli-
cating the matter still further is the very real possibility that some of
your forebears lived on more than one plantation and, as a consequence, may have been known by more than one slave owner's surname. You may have to rely on family oral history to ferret out the
surname(s) your forebears used during slavery. It is this very per-

sonal history that may contain clues about the particular plantation your ancestors lived on, which may lead you to the owner of this plantation. This history may also contain the actual surname of one or more plantation owners. If this information exists in your family's collective memory, some of the questions in chapter 4 will help you uncover it.

CONSIDERING FREE AFRICAN AMERICANS

Your discussions with relatives may have led you to believe that there is no history of slavery in your family. Although it will still be difficult to find the surnames you need, some help is available in the form of listings of African Americans who were free inhabitants of the United States even during slavery. The first U.S. census, taken in 1790, includes the names of free heads of African-American households. The census data also provides residence information, which may be invaluable if you know where your ancestors lived at the time the census was taken. If you have reason to believe your forebears were free inhabitants of the United States in 1790 and headed a household, you may find it helpful to consult *List of Free Black Heads of Families in the First Census of the United States, 1790* compiled by Debra L. Newman. This slim volume lists approximately four thousand free African-American heads of households. You can get a free copy of this publication by writing National Archives and Records Service, General Services Administration, Washington, D.C. Ask for Special List 34.

The data on which the list is based was collected in Connecticut, Delaware, Georgia, Kentucky, Maine, Maryland, Massachusetts, New Hampshire, New Jersey, New York, North Carolina, Pennsylvania, Rhode Island, South Carolina, Tennessee, Vermont, and Virginia. Information no longer exists for Georgia, Kentucky, New Jersey, and Tennessee. Data for Delaware and Virginia was reconstructed from state records.

Unfortunately, this listing of "free black heads of families" is not without its flaws, primarily because no standardized reporting procedure was used to collect the data. When accounting for free

African Americans in the population, some census takers listed only first names, along with the number in the household. Others recorded first names and indicated whether a particular person was black, Negro, mulatto, or free. Some listed no names at all, reporting only the race and the number of people in a household. We can be grateful, then, for those 1790 census takers who listed complete names of free African-American heads of households, including those precious surnames. From their work, we know, for example, that Sarah Hubbard of Connecticut headed a household of four; Winifred Wimbrey of North Carolina headed a household of seven; Thomas Babey of Maine headed a household of six; and Joseph Loyd of South Carolina headed a household of nine. You may be lucky enough to find the surnames you are looking for on this list. The possibility of such a discovery should encourage you to look through it.

There are other publications that identify African Americans who were free before the end of slavery. Among them are *Free Negro Heads of Families in the United States in 1830,* compiled by Carter G. Woodson, and *Free Negro Owners of Slaves in the United States in 1830 Together With Absentee Ownership of Slaves in the United States in 1830,* also compiled by Woodson (see bibliography). (It should be noted that some African Americans who are called slave owners were not such in the strictest sense. Those who could often bought their own relatives so that these relatives could be free.) The data in the Woodson volumes is organized by state and county. Therefore, if you know where your free forebears lived, the surnames listed in these volumes may trigger some memory or tie in with names that are part of your family's oral history.

Other publications about free African Americans in the antebellum period focus on particular states or regions of the country. One such publication is *The Free Negro in North Carolina, 1790–1860,* by historian John Hope Franklin. You may want to check with the librarian in your local or county library to determine if comparable materials are available for the state(s) in which your forebears lived. If so, you will want to consult these publications to determine if any of the surnames listed ring a bell and suggest follow-up.

Reviewing lists of names is slow, painstaking work that can be frustrating. Still, if the materials help you identify the surnames your forebears used, the work will be worth the effort and frustration.

You must not assume that your forebears were slaves simply because they lived in a slave state. Even during slavery, free African Americans lived south of the Mason-Dixon line. In 1860, for example, more than 260,000 free African Americans lived in the South.

UNDERSTANDING RACIAL DESIGNATIONS

As an African American, you will find some unexpected but solid help in gleaning information from public documents. Almost without fail, old records indicate the color of the person in question. For most documents, the name of a person of color is followed by a *C* or *Col* for colored; *M* for mulatto; or *B* for black. If you are looking for an African-American ancestor, the racial designation will help you in your search through public records.

During some periods in our history, racial designations were more precise. For example, enumerators for the 1890 census were instructed:

> Write white, black, mulatto, quadroon, octoroon, Chinese, Japanese, or Indian according to the color or race of the person enumerated. Be particularly careful to distinguish between blacks, mulattoes, quadroons, and octoroons. The word "black" should be used to describe those persons who have three-fourths or more black blood; "mulatto," those persons who have from three-eighths to five-eighths black blood; "quadroon," those persons who have one-fourth black blood; and "octoroon," those persons who have one-eighth or any trace of black blood.

It is unfortunate that most of the 1890 census was destroyed by fire. It would be interesting to know how enumerators met the challenge of distinguishing among people who had various amounts of "black" blood. At this late date, however, no African Americans intent on tracing their roots will be offended by this fixation with color. In fact, the practice of identifying people by race can be considered a powerful assist for the African-American genealogist. Those beautiful *B*s and *C*s sped my search for my roots more times than I can count.

Once you know the surnames you are looking for and understand how racial designations can help you, you are ready to consult official records that may be available to you in the towns and counties where your forebears were born. If your family has lived in the same place for generations, your search for information on its members may simply require a trip across town. You may find, however, that the records you need are located in other states. If your schedule and budget permit, visit some of the town halls and county courthouses in question. These visits may be more fruitful than you dared hope. If such excursions are impossible, however, you may be able to get some of the information you need by mail.

While you may know the names of the towns your forebears lived in, you may be uncertain which county courthouse holds records for each town. You might find it helpful to consult the *County Courthouse Book* by Elizabeth Petty Bentley, which includes addresses and phone numbers for more than three thousand county courthouses. The book also contains information about almost sixteen hundred towns and cities that maintain records comparable with those found in courthouses. (Again, check the bibliography.)

LOCATING BIRTH RECORDS

As important as birth records are, they are not always easy to find. According to the National Office of Vital Statistics, it was not until 1968 that 99.1 percent of live births were registered. Still, some of the earliest birth records for African Americans are those of slave births. For example, in 1804 New Jersey passed a gradual emancipation law, which mandated that female slaves born after July 4, 1804, were to be set free at age twenty-one. Male slaves born after that date were to be set free at age twenty-five. In compliance with the law, birth notifications were registered with county clerks throughout the state. Although surnames are rarely given, the documents, sometimes little more than poorly scribbled notes, do identify the slave mother, her child, and the slave owner's name and residence. This kind of information, replicated in courthouses and plantation records in many states, is sometimes enough to help find a forebear. Three such birth notifications, located in the Morris County, New Jersey, Court House, are shown below. The spelling, capitalization, and punctuation are those used in the notifications.

I certify that my negro female slave named Massey has delivered of a male Black child named Charles on the fifteenth day of April A.D. 1805 at my house in the township of Morris in the County of Morris. Witness my hand this thirtieth day of August A.D. 1812.—*Robert T. Kemble*

I Ezekiel Whitehead of the Township of Morris—Farmer—do certify that my negro female named Peg or Peggy was delivered of one birth of two children—the one a male child named Matt— and one female child named Loisa on the twenty seventh day of March A.D. Eighteen hundred and Eleven—at my house in the Township of Morris in the County of Morris aforesaid—Witness my hand at Morris Town—Jany. 9th A.D. 1812.—*Ezekiel Whitehead—Farmer*

I purchased of Charles A. O'Brine in the year of our Lord one thousand eight hundred & six a Negro Woman named Hannah with a Child called Phebe which is said to have been born on the twenty seventh day of October One Thousand eight hundred & five—The Mother of said Phebe named Hannah was on the 22d day of February 1808 delivered of a black Child cal'd Mary at my house which Child I gave to Betsy Wood at present the wife of James L. Hurd and on the 27th day of June 1810 the said Hannah was delivered of a female Child to the appearance of a mungrell breed which is named Dinah and on the 27th day of October in the Year of our lord one thousand eight hundred and twelve the said Hannah was delivered at my House of a Negro Boy (Black as jet) which is cal'd Jim. I do hereby certify the above or foregoing to be a true copy of the record of Blacks or People of Color belonging to my family excepting a Girl commonly caled Jiney or jin which I purchased of Amos Nicoles in June or July 1804 a slave for life as is also Hannah the first mentioned.—*Jn P. Losey*

Despite great strides in computerizing or microfilming documents, many birth records are still found in old ledgers or journals. Well into the twentieth century, doctors visited town halls or county courthouses whenever they had time to record the births of the children delivered since the last visit. First, the date the doctor actually registered the birth was recorded, making the birth registration later than the actual birth, sometimes by weeks. Then the child would be identified, perhaps only by sex, along with the name of the parents and the date and place of the actual birth. Sometimes doctors themselves would record this information in the ledger of births. At other times a clerk would enter into the ledger the information a doctor provided.

If you know the birth date of a particular forebear and the county and state in which this relative was born, you can often get a copy of the birth record by submitting a written request to the town or county clerk. You may find this helpful if the birth records you need are located in another state. Since some states kept separate records for whites and African Americans, specify the race of those about whom you are seeking information. According to the *Historical Statistics of the United States: Colonial Times to 1970,* "a newborn child is ordinarily assigned to the race of the parents. If parents are of different races, the following applies: (1) When only one parent is white, the child is assigned the other parent's race; (2) when neither is white, the child is assigned the father's race."

When writing for information, you are likely to meet with more success if you limit your request to one or two pieces of information. Town and county workers are likely to put aside requests for ten or fifteen different birth records until they can find a block of time to complete the search—and this block of time may be hard to come by. If, on the other hand, you are willing to wait for a response, request all the information you need.

Your letter, addressed to the clerk of the town or county in which your forebears were born, might read as follows:

Dear Sir or Madam:

> I am seeking a copy of the birth record of Henry Clark, who was born in Henrico County, Virginia, in the 1860s. He was an African American.
>
> I have enclosed a check for ten dollars ($10.00) to cover the cost of this transaction. If there are additional charges, please let me know.
>
> I thank you in advance for your kind consideration of this request.

If you are unsuccessful in obtaining a birth record from the town or county where a forebear was born, you can submit a written request for this information to the appropriate state office of vital records, using a letter comparable with the one shown above. State offices of vital records are listed in appendix I, along with addresses, telephone numbers, and the fees charged for each birth record you request. Some offices accept credit cards and even permit you to request information by fax.

Often, birth records became important to a family only when required for school enrollment. When this was the case, parents had to acquire something called a delayed birth certificate for their children. Many African Americans who migrated north in the 1930s and 1940s applied for these certificates so that they could enroll their children in northern schools. Each state has its own requirements for issuing delayed birth certificates. For example, in the 1940s—a period of significant African-American migration—the state of Georgia required any three of the following classes of evidence to issue a delayed birth certificate (records less than five years old were not accepted):

1. Baptismal, cradle roll, or other church record
2. Family Bible record

3. Physician's or hospital record of birth

4. Birth certificate of child

5. Record from a local, state, or federal census

6. School record

7. Insurance policy

8. Affidavit of relative or nonrelative

9. Affidavit of attending physician

10. Other acceptable records

The following agencies or officers in the state of Georgia were permitted to certify delayed birth certificates:

1. Georgia Department of Public Health

2. County or city health officers or registrars

3. County ordinary or clerk

4. Superior Court judge or clerk

If suitable proof was offered, a birth certificate was issued with the following statement:

The word "DELAYED" imprinted on the face of this document indicates that the original certificate was issued after a review of evidence presented by or in behalf of the subject of this certificate. This evidence conforms to the minimum standards set forth by the GEORGIA DEPARTMENT OF HEALTH. This certificate is generally accepted as proof of the facts stated thereon.

Some delayed birth certificates pose a particular problem for the genealogist. Often the names of the parents, including the mother's maiden name, are omitted. This may be because it is most often the parents who provide the necessary documentation for the officer who issues the certificate. Some officers therefore felt it unnecessary to identify the parents.

If you can determine what kinds of information were used to substantiate the birth, however, you may uncover family documents helpful to you. For example, if a family Bible was used as one proof of birth, you know a family Bible existed and probably still does. You can begin to search for it among your relatives. If a baptismal or other church record was used, you may be able to learn something about the church your forebears attended. Once you identify this church, you may find other records in it that will help you trace your roots. If census records were used to verify birth, you may be able to use these same records to learn the county or city where your forebears made their home.

My mother, who was born at home, needed an official record of her birth. After compiling and submitting the required information, the Georgia Department of Human Resources issued a delayed certificate of birth in 1980. The document lists the following as supporting evidence for issuance of the certificate and indicates the date of each document:

1. Affidavit made by mother (3/12/73)
2. Metropolitan Life Insurance Company policy (9/13/43)
3. Copy of application for Social Security (3/25/74)
4. Baptism record issued by Church of Our Lady of Mercy, Whippany, New Jersey (6/17/35)

Just as important, the delayed certificate of birth identifies my maternal grandparents and the county in Georgia where my mother was born. If I had not had access to this information already, it would have proved invaluable.

Delayed certificates of birth can be necessary for any number of reasons. My paternal grandfather and his siblings, all born at home in New Jersey, applied for delayed certificates so that they could qualify for Social Security benefits. The process for them was quite simple, since they still lived in the town of their birth. An older brother or sister simply accompanied the one seeking a birth certificate, took the family Bible—which contained family birth dates—identified their parents, and that was that. It probably helped that the town clerk knew the Thompsons as well as he knew his own family. There was no need to hassle anyone about something as simple as when and where she was born when the information was common knowledge.

In general, you will find most states more than accommodating when receiving requests for delayed birth certificates. For example, anyone born or residing in Florida who wishes to apply for a delayed birth certificate must first submit to the County Court in the county of birth or residence, a statement from the official custodian of birth records of the state of birth that no certificate has been filed. Once that is done, at least three of the documents listed below must be submitted to the County Court.

1. Certified copy of a school record
2. Old family Bible
3. Baptismal record
4. Certified copy of application for a marriage license
5. Military record
6. Driver's license or voter's registration card, at least five years old
7. Old insurance policy
8. Birth certificate of child
9. Affidavit of physician, midwife or person older than the petitioner who has definite knowledge of petitioner's birth
10. Copy of federal census record
11. Any other convincing evidence

If you have older relatives who, for some reason, do not have records of their birth, encourage them to apply for a delayed certificate. Some may not know that it is possible to acquire this document. The information uncovered in the process may be helpful to you, and it will certainly be helpful to your descendants. Remember to record all birth information and other facts found in birth records on your Individual Family Worksheets. Equally important, keep in mind that you may well be visiting the town or county where family records are found. If this is the case, you can search through these records yourself. By doing so, you may discover other information in public records that will help you trace your roots—information that would not be sent to you in response to your request for specific birth records.

FINDING MARRIAGE RECORDS

Marriage records, usually found in the town hall or courthouse of the city or county where the marriage took place, can provide even more information than birth records. The certificates and records of marriage issued in the early part of the twentieth century usually indicate race, place of birth, occupation, and parents of both the bride and groom. In addition, the marriage site and name of the person officiating are also shown. Just consider what a wealth of information this is if you are seeking your roots—all of it on a single document. Older marriage records can yield even more surprises and some much-needed help.

In my own search, census records and an old deed told me that my paternal great-great-grandmother's given name was Stacia. She was always known by her married name, Stacia Thompson. Census records further showed that she had both a daughter and a granddaughter named Stacia. So the *Stacia* part seemed firm, even though church records listed her name as *Estacia*. In truth, the spelling of her first name, with or without an *E,* simply didn't matter. What did matter, however, was her maiden name. No one in the family knew what it was. Yet only through this name would I be able to identify another branch of my family.

After a little digging, I discovered that the marriage records for Morris County, the county in which Stacia Thompson lived, dating from the mid- to late 1800s were stored in the county clerk's office. This meant I had a chance to find a record of her marriage; thankfully, it had not been stored in our town hall, which burned to the ground in 1919, consuming many family birth, marriage, and death records in its blaze. At the county offices a clerical worker directed me to the index of marriages that covered the period of time I believed my great-great-grandparents were married. According to census records, he was born in 1820; she was born in 1825. Based on these dates, I guessed that the earliest they would have been married was sometime in the 1840s.

In the *Liber of Marriages from April 20, 1841 to October 7, 1863*, I found a wonderful listing, alphabetized according to the name of the groom. My heart raced a little as I sped toward the *T*s. This couldn't be so simple. But it was. There, written in someone's clear hand, was my paternal great-great-grandfather's name, Charles A. Thompson. He married, the entry said, Anastacia Anderson. Anastacia, not Stacia, and—gift of all gifts—Anderson. Since the listing said nothing about color, though, I feared I might have the wrong Charles and Stacia. The reference continued, directing me to section 2 of the marriage records, page 189.

Hurrying to that section and page, I found: "Charles Thompson, Anastacia Anderson, Pequannac, September 29, 1849. Colored." The records also gave me a clue about the location of the Anderson home. Pequannac is an area quite close to Whippany, where Charles Thompson lived. Charles and Anastacia were married by the Reverend J. L. Janeway. In addition to indicating that Charles and Anastacia were "colored," the reverend provided the following information for the records of marriages in Morris County, New Jersey, that he performed between 1848 and 1850: "The above were performed whilst I was pastor of the church at Montville, Morris County and the marriages took place in the county. I add the Name of the church—1st R. Dutch at Montville as I am not certain about the law on this point." Montville, the site of the church, is less than five miles from Whippany.

Handling these old handwritten records was a heady experience. I could actually feel their importance. When I learned that the ledgers would soon be taken out of circulation so the information they contained could be microfilmed, I decided to see if I could find marriages of other family members. I did! Among them were these, performed by the Reverend Charles C. Parker, pastor of the Presbyterian Church in Parsippany, Morris County, New Jersey:

> This is to certify that on the Fourteenth day of June A.D 1873 at Parsippany township of Hanover County of Morris and State of New Jersey I united in Holy Matrimony Henry Conover (colored) aged thirty-two of Morristown, N.J., son of John Conover to Mistress Caroline Baker (colored) aged twenty-six of Morristown, New Jersey, daughter of James Baker. . . .

> This is to certify that on the first day of April, A.D. 1875 at Troy Township in Hanover, county of Morris and State of New Jersey I united in Holy Matrimony Matthew W. Wright (colored) aged thirty five of Montville County and State aforementioned, son of James Wright to Harriet Ann Conover (colored) aged nineteen of Troy aforesaid daughter of John Conover. . . .

The John Conover mentioned in both instances is my paternal great-great-great grandfather. Further, the ages given for his children verified the birth information about Henry and Harriet Ann recorded in the Conover family Bible.

Marriage records can help verify any number of other records and, just as important, family oral history. My own family's oral history indicated that we have been connected to the Wright family for more than a hundred years. Finding the marriage record of Harriet Ann Conover and Matthew Wright explained for the first time how this connection came about.

If the marriage records you seek are located in another state, you can write for the information using a letter similar to the one suggested for acquiring birth information (see page 92). Again, do not despair if your appeal to town or county officers turns up nothing. The appropriate state office of vital records may be able to provide the marriage documentation you need. To get the information, again, simply follow the procedures described for obtaining birth records (see page 92). Appendix I includes a listing of the fees charged for copies of marriage records; it also specifies the years for which marriage records are available. Remember to make your requests specific. If you can identify the race of the people you are seeking information on, the search at the state level may be faster. Do not forget to record all marriage information into your research notebooks on the Individual Family Worksheets.

ACQUIRING DEATH RECORDS

Like the registration of births, registration of deaths on a national level was slow to arrive. In 1900 only ten states routinely required that deaths be registered. By 1933 all states (forty-eight at the time) required registration of death. Still, in some areas deaths are believed to have been underreported.

As I mentioned above, it was customary to record deaths in family Bibles. Sometimes the notation is so precise as to be painful. Family members often recorded not only the month and day but also the hour and minute death occurred. Family Bible records are not always as precise as to the place of death, however. This might be indicated simply as "at home," which is not unusual for deaths that preceded the advent and general acceptance of hospitals. Nor do these records often help you learn the cause of death—not surprising, since medical diagnosis may not have been available to family members. If deaths have been recorded in your family Bible, you will, of course, transfer them to your Individual Family Worksheets. As with birth and marriage records, begin your search for death records in the town or county where the forebear you are researching died. The quantity of information provided on Certificates and Records of Death is impressive. When records include an identification by race, African Americans find a strong assist in matching the information to forebears.

Death records are fully as helpful as marriage records. My paternal great-great-grandfather Charles Thompson died on May 19, 1895, while visiting relatives in Newark, New Jersey. His death record lists his birthplace, residence, and burial location as Whippany, New Jersey, which I already knew, but the spaces for the names of his parents, which I had hoped for, are blank. Charles's youngest son, William, died in 1927. His death certificate, issued by the County Board of Health, lists his residence, the place of his death, his age to the day, and, of course, his race. It includes his occupation (brickyard laborer), birthplace, and parents (Stacia and Charles Thompson, although the informant, a nephew-in-law, did not know Stacia's maiden name). The death certificate also notes where his parents were born, the cause of William's death, the medical attendant, the place and date of burial, and the name and address of the undertaker. Again, a wealth of data that helped me substantiate information in the Thompson family Bible and in his military records.

Because much of the information contained in Certificates and Records of Death is provided by a family member or friend, you must be careful about accepting it all without verification. Sometimes family members do not want to divulge "family business" to strangers. For example, a parent may be listed as "unknown" if the death certificate is for someone believed to have been conceived out of wedlock. The age shown in a given death record may be wrong simply because the informant did not know the age of the deceased. The place of birth may be guessed at. Still a death record gives you something to go on and places to check. You are ahead of the game for every significant Certificate and Record of Death your research uncovers.

You should remember that a death record can help you document information about forebears from a much earlier time. For example, my great-great-grandmother Elsy Conover Deree died in 1924, after the Whippany town hall fire. Therefore, I found a record of her death in the town clerk's office. This death record includes the names and birthplaces of her parents (my great-great-great-grandparents), including her mother's maiden name. Using this information, I was able to trace the Conover branch of my family back to 1817.

SEARCHING THROUGH PROBATE COURT RECORDS

Wills, deeds, and records regarding the distribution of property and appointment of guardians are among the documents found in probate court holdings. These documents contain information—especially family names—that you may not find in other places. If such documents have not been destroyed or lost, you can usually acquire copies of them by submitting a written request to the probate court in question.

Wills

For African Americans tracing their roots, two kinds of wills are important. First, of course, are the wills our own forebears left specifying how their worldly goods were to be parceled out. Although beneficiaries are the primary focus of most wills, sometimes the parents of the person making the will or parents of beneficiaries who may be minor children are identified. You will find that a description of property to be divided can be very helpful, especially if that property is land: The description of land and its location can take you back to a family home place.

If you visit probate offices, you should take advantage of the opportunity to read all the wills that pertain to members of your family. This may take several days, but if you are willing to invest the time, you may find that your investment pays off handsomely. A will may indicate bequests to people whose names are unfamiliar to you. Because these names may lead you to other important information about your family, note them for follow-up.

While wills of forebears are important in finding your way back to your earliest African-American ancestors, the wills of slave owners may be even more helpful. Slaves were considered valuable property. If a man owned slaves, those slaves were often mentioned in his will and left to his heirs, along with houses, livestock, and other possessions. When you are trying to find forebears by using wills left by slave or plantation owners, two pieces of information are crucial. The first is surnames; this time, however, it is the slave or plantation owner's surname that you are looking for. And the second is place-names—the names of the state and county in which the plantation owner lived and, perhaps, the name of the plantation.

You may well have to tap into your family's oral history to help you locate the wills left by slave owners. Perhaps one relative remembers a state where your forebears lived. Another may remember a slave owner's name, or a plantation name or a county name. Someone may know the name of a forebear who spent time in slavery. He may only be able to come up with a first name; still, that first name can serve you very nicely since most wills, if they named slaves at all, contained only the first names of slaves being transferred. Armed with this kind of information, you are well on your way to deciphering whatever keys to your past exist in the wills of slave and plantation owners.

It was not unusual for a slave owner to include in her will that some or all of the slaves she owned would be granted freedom upon her death. If your forebears obtained freedom in this way, you may discover that they became free inhabitants of the United States long before slavery was abolished in this country. In this case, you may be able to find them listed in the census population schedules, discussed in chapter 7.

Probate records often include an inventory of the estate, made after the estate owner's death. These inventories are usually quite complete, listing every possession down to the last hoe and piece of silverware. Such records also contain information that may be of value to you as you trace your roots. For example, if the estate was sold, probate records identify the new owner. If the estate included slaves, these slaves were often transferred to the new owner and required to take his surname. You know how vital this information about surnames is to your search. Every pertinent surname you uncover takes you closer to your earliest African-American ancestors.

If you know the location of the plantation your forebears lived on and the name of its owner, you can write to the clerk of the probate court in question and request a copy of the plantation owner's will, which may contain the information about your earliest African-American ancestors. Wills can be lengthy documents, so you may want to learn in advance the fee for duplication. If you know the name of the plantation on which your forebears spent time, you may want to visit the county in which it was located to review wills and other documents yourself. If you decide to do this, make copies of all the wills that contain information you believe may be helpful to you. Having copies in your possession will permit you to study the documents more carefully when time permits. Careful scrutiny of documents often calls your attention to information you overlooked in a cursory reading.

With ever-increasing frequency, court records and documents are being computerized. Granted, progress toward complete computerization of these records is slower than we would wish. Still, you may find that some of the courthouses you visit will have a computerized index that lists all references to a given person's estate recorded in various court documents. The prospect of having to check only one index is exciting.

Deeds

Deeds are important not only because they identify forebears but also because they identify home places. Deeds are normally indexed in two ways: by the name of the grantee (buyer) and by the name of the grantor (seller). You therefore have two chances to locate deeds that apply to property your forebears bought or sold. As with wills, deeds also record the transfer of slaves. As a consequence, locating a deed may help you discover forebears who were unknown to you or even the very ones you are searching for.

Again, surnames are key to finding the deeds in which you are interested. Once you have these surnames and have located the deeds, make a copy of them or record all the important information they contain. This information includes the date on the deed and the date it was filed; the buyers and sellers of the property in question; the price paid for the property; when the property was purchased; and where it is located. In case you need to refer to the deed again, note the volume the deed was recorded in and the page number(s) on which it can be found.

It is also important to record all the information that pertains to the transfer of slaves. Of course, you will record the names of these slaves, even if only first names are listed. If ages of slaves being transferred are listed, record these as well; if the slaves turn out to be ancestors, their ages will help you determine birth dates that may be unavailable elsewhere. Sometimes deeds indicate distinguishing characteristics or skills possessed by the slaves being transferred. Note these as well. For example, if a slave being transferred is a cabinetmaker or seamstress and you believe her to be a forebear, you may be able to track her by this skill as she moves to other plantations or out of slavery.

Although a slave's name was often changed when he was sold, his particular talent or skill is likely to have been noted in plantation records of the new owner. If those records still exist, you may be able to find him by looking for a slave with his particular talent. When your forebear attained freedom, he may have changed his name yet once more. Still, his talent or skill is likely to have become his occupation, which will be noted in census records. Those records will also identify members of his family whose names will be familiar to you or to a relative. You will read more about tracking your forebears by using plantation and census records later in this book.

Tax Records

If your ancestors owned property, they will have paid taxes on it. Your search through family documents or court records may have uncovered deeds specifying the property owned or wills indicating how property was transferred. Or perhaps you have neither deed nor will, but you do have an abundance of family oral history that suggests your forebears owned a "piece of land" in a particular place. If you can identify this place, records in the tax assessor's office may help you find out more about your forebears.

Ferreting out old tax records is not always easy. Sometimes older tax records are located in basements or warehouses. Still, if you can find them, you may be able to learn, specifically, where your forebears lived and how long they lived there. Among my family documents are copies of tax records that list quarterly tax payments on Block 8702, Lot 4—the current designation for the land acquired by Charles and Stacia Thompson in 1868. If it had been necessary for me to go to the local tax assessor's office to find these tax records, though, I would have been guided by the surname *Thompson*. There I would find the property designated as the estate of

A. M. Thompson. In fact the estate is that of A. *W.* Thompson, or Ann Williams Thompson, my great-grandmother. It became her estate upon the death of her husband, Edward, who, as Charles and Stacia's oldest son, inherited their property. Some clerk misread the *W* for an *M,* and the *M* has stayed all these years. Still, my family knows the proper designation and no one has ever seen any reason to hassle the tax officer into changing it.

African-American ownership of property in this country goes back to the 1600s, when the first black indentured servants, once their time of indenture was over, began to acquire property of their own. Exploring old tax records may reveal information that will help you trace your roots back to early property owners in this country—who just may be your forebears.

OVERCOMING HANDWRITING PITFALLS

When neither word processors nor typewriters were available, the legibility and accuracy of written records depended on the handwriting and conscientiousness of the person who wrote them. Even when the information in old records is transcribed correctly, the handwriting can be difficult to decipher. Had the clerk who recorded my great-great-grandparents' marriage—he signed his name, Stanburrough, with all the appropriate flourishes underneath—not written with a clear hand, I might never have been able to decipher his information. On the other hand, I can barely read the transcription of the deed recorded by a clerk whose own name I cannot make out. If the original deed were not in my possession, I would know very little about the property my Thompson forebears acquired in 1868.

Your success in tracing your roots will depend at least in part on your ability to decipher handwritten information that seems, at first glance, to be illegible. In fairness to all those clerks who labored day after day, copying document after document in dimly lit spaces, I must admit that I have sometimes written things myself that I cannot decipher just a few days, or even a few hours, later.

Deciphering handwritten information about your forebears may require some effort. The first and most important rule in doing this is to take your time. Eventually, you will learn to discriminate between letters that look alike. When I began my research, I found it difficult to tell if a given letter was a capital *I* or a capital *J.* Sometimes the *S* in Stacia looked very much like an *L.* At other times the *T* in Thompson seemed to be an *F.* One of the things that helped me most was looking at different records. The census enumerator who took the 1860 census in the Whippany section of Hanover Township was a man named William McClearty. Mr. McClearty wrote with a firm, clear hand. Since my Thompson, Conover, and Williams forebears stayed put, I could compare the 1860 census records with those of 1850 and 1870, which were compiled by enumerators who wrote less clearly. This exercise helped me understand various handwriting foibles.

I also found it helpful to look at information in context. Sometimes the handwriting became clear as I began to make sense of specific sentences or phrases that were repeated throughout a document. As difficult as it seems at first, you will get the knack of deciphering documents written long ago. You may find it helpful to consult *How to Read the Handwriting and Records of Early America* by Kate Kirkham.

DEALING WITH SPELLING DILEMMAS

Once you have deciphered the documents that include names or residences of your forebears, you may be thrown off track by the spelling of those names and places. There was a time in this country when you could spell a word just about any way you pleased. Throughout much of the nineteenth century, people often spelled names, places, and things the way they sounded. Old records are full of these phonetic spellings.

The racial designations once so prevalent in public records may help you get past this spelling dilemma. When you look at the spellings of surnames, use this powerful assist, and use your imagination to *hear* the spelling. For example, I believe the correct spelling of my great-great-grandmother's maiden name is *Anderson*;

this is the spelling I have found most often in documents that refer to her. However, the name has also been spelled *Anndersin, Andursan, Anndirson.* Luckily, these spellings were always preceded by some form of *Stacia* and always followed by some racial designation indicating that she was African American. As I learned more about her—her birth year, her marriage date, her status as a property owner, her church membership—the various spellings no longer caused a problem.

During your research, take down all the spellings of the surname that could possibly apply to the forebear you are looking for. With time, patience, and work, things will sort themselves out.

UNDERSTANDING THE RELATIONSHIPS

My paternal great-grandmother Ann Williams Thompson was one of seven children. Among them was her brother Curnell Ellsworth Williams. This brother named one of his own sons Curnell Ellsworth, who in turn named one of his sons Curnell Ellsworth. This gives us three Curnell Ellsworths. (Clearly, we've got a good thing going here.) Perhaps because she ran out of names, my great-grandmother named her ninth child, my grandfather, Curnell Ellsworth. Therefore, in my family the name *Curnell Ellsworth* can refer to a father, a son, a brother, an uncle, a nephew, a great-nephew, or a cousin. Obviously, the most important forebear in terms of my research has been my paternal grandfather Curnell Ellsworth Thompson. All the others carry the surname Williams.

Still, some family documents only refer to Curnell, or Uncle El (a nickname my father first used to refer to his mother's brother but one that was later used to refer to other Curnell Ellsworths). Until I discovered the birth dates of the various Curnell Ellsworths, gleaned primarily from census records, family Bibles, and death records, I was hard pressed to tell some Curnell Ellsworths from others. But an embarrassment of Curnells is not the only name problem my family has.

My father's name was Leonard Leroy Thompson. His first son was named for him. This son died shortly after birth, and eleven years later a second son was born to my parents. This son, my brother, was named Leonard Leroy Thompson III (normally a designation that would suggest he is my father's grandson, not his son). My brother had a son of his own whom he named (of course) Leonard IV and who, in turn, had a son named Leonard V. As you can see, we are in danger of creating our own Curnell crisis for those who follow us.

When you talk with relatives, study family documents, and research public records, do not assume a particular relationship for all those who bear the same given names or even the same surnames. In certain geographical areas, some surnames are common and some given names are popular. A few of the Thompsons I found, while African American and while sharing a given name with a known relative, are not related to me. Study the information available to you and verify it with other sources before offering someone a place on your family genealogy chart. While minor relatives will try to lay claim to your time and attention, your primary focus should be on parents, grandparents, great-grandparents, great-great grandparents, and so on, in a direct line. These are the forebears who will take you back to the ancestors who established your family in this country.

6

Investigating Church
Records and Cemeteries

The close ties between African Americans and religion are
well documented. Your family's oral history is probably
full of "church stories," which may include your forebears'
earliest religious experiences in this country. Records of those experiences, including transfers from one congregation to another, may
provide valuable information that will help you in your search for
your earliest African-American ancestors. If some of your forebears
were slaves, their first religious experiences in this country may have
been attending worship services with a plantation owner and his
family. Even if there is no history of slavery in your family, some of
your ancestors may have attended churches where most of these
congregants were white, often because no other churches were
available to them or within traveling distance. When whites and
African Americans worshiped together, a certain part of the sanctuary was often set aside for African Americans. Even the church
door, it seems, was not strong enough to bar segregation.

If yours is a churchgoing family, recent church records may contain information about your parents, grandparents, or great-grandparents that is missing from your Individual Family Worksheets. Older church records, especially those up to and including the mid–nineteenth century, can yield a wealth of information about your earlier African-American foreparents—information that may be available nowhere else. Some church records contain not only the names of African-American worshipers but information about when they were born and baptized, as well. Baptismal data can be especially important, because slave owners sometimes freed slaves upon baptism, continuing a practice that was fairly common in this nation's early colonial period. Even if a slave was not manumitted upon baptism, however, records of baptism often contain the name of the slave owner. Adding the slave owner's surname to the name and location of the church and the name and age of the person being baptized may help you find an early African-American forebear. In this instance, the quantity of information is substantial enough to help you find that forebear even if baptismal records contain only a first name.

Church records also contain information about confirmations, marriages, deaths, and burials. Marriage records usually include the names and ages of the couple being wed, the date of the marriage, and the wedding site. Those identified as witnesses to this rite may be forebears who were unknown to you. When church records include death data, this data often specifies the location of the burial site, which may be a church cemetery or even a private family burial place. If your forebears were buried in a church cemetery, they may have been assigned to the "colored" section of that cemetery. In some places separation of the races, even in death, continued well into the twentieth century. If your forebears were interred in a private cemetery, it may be on property that was part of a plantation or estate. If this is the case, you can be fairly certain that the forebear buried there had some connection with the plantation owners—most likely one based on slavery. Consequently, finding a burial site may well take you directly to one of the plantations your forebears worked on as slaves. The records of this plantation, if they still exist, may enable you to find your earliest African-American ancestors. (You will read more about examining plantation records in chapter 8.)

FINDING CHURCH RECORDS

To locate church records that may provide information about your forebears, you will have to determine which church or denomination these forebears belonged to. A good way to start your research in this area is to think about current family religious affiliations. If most members of your family are Methodists or Baptists or Roman Catholics, they are likely to have been so for some time. If members of your family changed denominations, perhaps leaving the Methodist Church to become Presbyterians or the Baptist Church to become Muslims, you may find written documentation of these changes among your family papers. Sometimes churches grant certificates to new members, certifying the date when membership in the congregation became effective. In other cases stories of changes in church affiliation may be part of your family's oral history, especially if these changes caused conflict within the family. Interesting and informative stories may be attached to these changes.

You can also find clues about the family's church affiliation by looking through old church bulletins or programs issued when a family member was baptized, confirmed, wed, or eulogized. These rites are most often carried out in the church that the family attended. You may have already discovered a few such church bulletins when you were collecting information about your family. Now would be a good time to look through them further, noting the names of the pastors. These clergy members may be able to add to the information you have already collected and suggest additional sources that may be helpful to you in identifying your family's church affiliations.

Funeral cards or programs usually identify the church in which the burial service in question was held. The deceased may well have been affiliated with this particular church, or had some association with its pastor. The program often lists former residences and church affiliations for the deceased, too, which may help you pinpoint a site of family religious activities. Hold on to funeral programs. They are likely to include information beyond church affiliation, including the birthplace of the deceased, birth and death dates, and the names of parents and other relatives. Some indication of employment or occupation may be given, and membership in social and civic organizations noted. The organizations a forebear belonged to may well have records that can facilitate your research.

Finally, funeral cards usually indicate the time and place of internment. This may be the only information you have about the burial site for this family member. You may well find other forebears interred in the same place. If you have not already done so, take a few minutes to record all of the information found on funeral cards on the appropriate Individual Family Worksheet.

Your family Bible may also contain information about your family's church affiliations. For example, if a forebear was baptized at home, the Bible may give the name of the minister or priest who performed the baptism and indicate the church represented. In addition to providing the names of the bride and groom, Bible entries for marriages may name the church where these marriages were performed. Death entries may be followed by the site of the burial service, which may be the church attended by the deceased. The burial site itself may be on church grounds. Obituaries printed in newspapers may name the church in which funeral services were held. Although you are concentrating on trying to identify church affiliations, remember that obituaries often provide other important family information about the deceased: the name of the surviving spouse and children, birthplace, birth and death dates, parents and other relatives, religious and civic associations, and occupation. Be sure to record this information on the appropriate Individual Family Worksheets.

When you are trying to determine your family's religious affiliations, talk with older members of your family. Ask them to recount their earliest memories of churchgoing and the oldest stories they remember about the family's church activities. Perhaps your family's oral history will contain stories of attending religious services in a chapel on a plantation where the family may have lived. Or your family's history may include stories of secret religious meetings held during slavery and attended at the end of long days of hard work or when the slave owner was away from the plantation. Perhaps old hymns and gospel songs hold clues about your family's early religious experiences in this country.

If you are lucky, you will be able to identify a few of the churches your forebears attended. If you are very lucky, records will exist in these churches that can help you trace your roots to a particular time and place. An element of luck really is necessary here. Some churches kept no records. Other churches and the records they contained were destroyed. In some instances church records were kept by itinerant preachers, who carried these records with them from church to church and ultimately filed them away somewhere in their own homes or destroyed them when they appeared to serve no further purpose. In too many cases old church records were considered unimportant and, as a consequence, were improperly maintained, if maintained at all. Sometimes church records were disposed of to make room for other church documents.

Still, do not be discouraged. Church records are worth looking for and through. While you may not want to spend a lifetime trying to locate church records that apply to your family, be on the lookout for them. They may turn up when and where you least expect to find them.

Once you have identified the church or churches in which your family worshiped, you are ready to find out if the records you need still exist. First contact the pastors of the churches your family attended. Either they will know where existing church records are located, or they will be able to identify an older church member who may know where records are kept. Some churches have turned their records over to the archival centers for their particular denomination. The Presbyterian Historical Society in Philadelphia, for example, houses records for many Presbyterian churches. Although some archival holdings less than fifty years old are restricted, you will be given access to earlier records. It is, in fact, these earlier records that may help you find information about your Presbyterian forebears available nowhere else.

A number of state archives, historical centers, and universities have also been chosen as custodians for certain church records. The United Methodist Archives and History Center, for example, is located at Drew University in Madison, New Jersey. These archives are largely computerized, and the collection can be accessed by computer modem. You can either use your own computer or one at a library to determine if these holdings include information about your Methodist forebears.

There are other sources that may yield information about the church(es) your ancestors attended. From 1939 to 1941 the Works Projects Administration (WPA) collected information on African-American churches and on white churches that accepted African-American members. These records are usually available in state libraries, archives, or historical societies. Do not hesitate to write or telephone the archivist at your state resource center (see appendix II) to determine if one of these depositories has records of the church(es) you are interested in. If these records exist, one of the archivists will know about them and be able to point you in the right direction.

You may also find valuable information about your forebears' church affiliations among two collections sometimes overlooked by African-American genealogists as viable research sources. The first is the collection maintained by the Society of Friends, or Quakers. The Quakers keep very careful membership records, including those that pertain to births, marriages, and deaths. You can find historical records of this group in the *Encyclopedia of American Quaker Genealogy,* by William Wade Hinshaw. The six volumes of this work contain genealogical data from the late 1600s to the mid-1920s, gathered from records of Quaker meetings (congregations) in six states: New Jersey, New York, North Carolina, Ohio, Pennsylvania, and Virginia. These volumes are available in many libraries that have genealogical collections. You may want to keep in mind two interesting facts about the Quakers. First, at their yearly meeting in 1796, the Quakers resolved that prospective members should be admitted to their number without regard to color. Second, and just as important, Quakers were active and effective conductors on the Underground Railroad, helping countless African Americans escape from slavery.

A second collection that may be helpful to you in identifying your forebears' religious experiences is found at the Family History Library established by members of the Church of Jesus Christ of Latter-day Saints, commonly known as the Mormons. The Family History Library is the largest genealogical collection in the world. Believing that family relationships are eternal, members are obligated to trace family roots as far back as possible. The library, located in Salt Lake City, Utah, has almost two million rolls of microfilm that contain, among a wealth of other information, church and burial records. The Family History Library catalog is available on CD-ROM and microfiche and lists the materials that are available either on loan or in the Salt Lake City facilities.

You need not visit the library in Utah to take advantage of some of its holdings; a number of local centers are located throughout the country. You can find the address of the local Family History Library nearest you in your public library or by writing to the Family History Library, 35 North West Temple Street, Salt Lake City, UT 84150. A visit to a local Family History Library branch will help you determine if the library holdings can help you identify your ancestors' religious affiliations or uncover other information about them. You should know that African Americans are well represented in the library's holdings. Among these holdings are birth, death, and marriage records; tax and census data; newspapers; court records; and military records. The library also has a large collection of Freedmen's Bureau records (discussed in chapter 8).

The Family History Library also maintains the United States Social Security Death Index on CD-ROM. The information contained in this database, although incomplete, dates from about 1935. Using the name of a deceased forebear, you can discover his birth and death dates, where his Social Security card was issued, and where he lived when he died. Your local Social Security office will be able to provide more complete information, such as birthplace, employment information, spouse's name, and perhaps parents' names, if you can prove your relationship to the forebear in question and can provide his Social Security number. Working through your local Social Security office will probably take more time, however, than tapping into the Family History Library database.

Although the Family History Library contains a number of printed family histories, you will want to make sure that any family that bears your surname really is your family. A careful check of all the data you have collected thus far will help you make this determination. Further, as with all materials supplied to databases by individuals, you will want to verify the information you believe pertains to your forebears to the extent that this is possible.

REVEALING FAMILY HISTORY

On April 12, 1860, "Estacia Thompson (colored) presented herself as a candidate for admission to the church. After a usual examination, she was declared approved." Thus began an unbroken line of Thompson family membership in the First Presbyterian Church in Whippany, New Jersey, that continues to this day. I've always wondered why my great-great-grandmother chose to be the first African American to join with that congregation. Ten years later her husband, Charles, along with several others, "presented themselves for examination as candidates for admission to the church. After prayer by Elder Cook, the candidates were examined as to their Christian experience and hope in Christ. And on motion were unanimously [elected] to the fellowship and ordinances of the church." Obviously my great-great-grandfather was left to hold the fort, because Stacia was "dismissed [transferred] to the African-Methodist Episcopal Church in Morristown, New Jersey," shortly after her husband joined the Presbyterian ranks.

Family oral history says that Charles joined the Presbyterian Church because he was offered a job as church sexton—a job restricted to congregation members. Perhaps that is why he stayed on after Stacia departed. He was not left alone for long, however.

On August 23, 1872, his oldest son, Edward, married Ann Elizabeth Williams in the church sanctuary. Births, baptisms, marriages, applications for church membership, deaths, and burials of the Thompsons, all identified by color and most by age, are well documented in the records of the Whippany Presbyterian Church. Two volumes of church history, worn with age, the inked inscriptions now brown, reveal a great deal about my Thompson forebears. Fortunately, and quite recently, these volumes were microfilmed and the microfilm sent to the Presbyterian Historical Society in Philadelphia. Should any of our descendants wish to consult these records, they will be available.

In addition to helping me verify dates and relationships, church records indicate that the Whippany congregation was sympathetic to the plight of African Americans. Minutes from November 1838 include the following: "Resolved that the Reverend Geo. Finney, agent of the American Anti-Slavery Society be invited to deliver a lecture on the subject of the abolition of slavery at his convenience." And on December 12, 1869 the minutes include: "It was voted that . . . the cause of the Freedmen be presented for aid on Sabbath morning of the 19th."

While my Thompson and Williams forebears were Presbyterian, my Conover ancestors were Roman Catholics. They attended St. Mary's Catholic Church in Belleville, New Jersey, and then Our Lady of Mercy Catholic Church in Whippany. I always wondered if my great-grandparents Nancy and John Conover named their offspring after members of these Roman Catholic congregations: John, Maud, Mary, Harold, Michael, Elizabeth, Gladys, Bridget, Patrick. Records of births, first confessions, first communions, marriages (inside and outside the rail), and internments in Catholic cemeteries mark the life and passing of countless Conovers. Also noted are those Catholic Conovers who bolted. My great-great-grandmother Elsy marched herself into the Whippany Presbyterian Church to marry a man whose name appears just this once. No records remain to tell where he came from or what happened to him after his wedding day. My paternal grandmother and my mother, both Roman Catholics, did what was expected of them when they decided to marry Thompsons: They married in the Presbyterian Church and became Presbyterians.

My own young years were made more memorable by visits from nuns, especially during Holy Week, who came to our home specifically to assure my mother that she was going straight to hell and her children with her if she did not return with us to the true church. It was this "true church," by virtue of its record keeping, that provided some of the documentation my mother needed to get a delayed birth certificate.

The oldest organized black church in the United States also has some records of value to those seeking to trace their roots. Philadelphia's Bethel African Methodist Episcopal Church was founded by Richard Allen on June 10, 1794. The Historical Society of Pennsylvania holds among its collections copies of the *Christian Recorder*, the official publication of the Bethel Church. Although many of the church's records and files were lost or destroyed, the *Christian Recorder* contains information about African Americans from various parts of the country, dating from 1856.

With careful searching and luck you may be able to find church records that will take you closer to your ancestors. While carrying out this exploration, take time to update the record of your family's religious affiliations and activities. Keep all bulletins that record rites or ceremonies your family takes part in. Collect church information from other family members and relatives. Make a special place among your documents for church programs or mementos. And of course record church affiliations on the appropriate Individual Family Worksheets. Your descendants will thank you.

EXPLORING CEMETERIES

A crumbling tombstone in the graveyard of the First Presbyterian Church in Woodbridge, New Jersey, commemorates the death of a slave named Jack, who died in 1825. The epitaph reads: "IN MEMORY OF JACK, A COLORD [SIC] MAN WHO BELONGED TO JONATHAN FREEMAN. HE WAS A FAITHFUL SERVANT & DIED JULY 23, 1825 IN THE 43RD YEAR OF HIS AGE." In 1998 the mostly white congregation of the Woodbridge church, in cooperation with the local historical association, raised enough money to replace Jack's tombstone. Although other cemetery plots are near Jack's now, it is clear that his burial site was once separated from the main graveyard. All other tombstones from this period are thirty to seventy-five yards away.

A second African American, Corporal Joseph Williams, a Civil War soldier who served in Company A of the Fourth U.S. Colored Infantry, is buried next to Jack in the Woodbridge cemetery. There is no indication, however, as to when Corporal Williams was born, died, or was buried. Like Corporal Williams, many military men are buried in private cemeteries, some resting under headstones supplied by the U.S. government under the terms of an act passed in 1879. If one or more of your forebears served in the military, one of his relatives may have applied for a headstone to mark his burial site. Other forebears of yours who served in the military may have been buried in national cemeteries. Data about headstone applications and military burials is available in the National Archives. These records include the name of the veteran and the place and date of burial. An archivist at your regional archive branch will be able to help you locate these records if you believe they can be of help to you. You will find a listing of the regional branches of the National Archives in appendix III.

Locating Cemeteries

There are several different kinds of cemeteries, and you may need to explore more than one to find the burial places of your ancestors. Some are church cemeteries. These are sometimes found on property adjacent to the church to which they belong; at other times church cemeteries are located on land that, while some distance from the church, has been acquired and set aside for church burials. Public cemeteries are just that—cemeteries owned by a city or town and maintained with taxpayer money. Private cemeteries, on the other hand, are developed and maintained as profit-making enterprises. A fourth kind of cemetery, the family cemetery, is usually located on land owned by a particular family. Burial in these cemeteries is usually limited to family members or to those the family wished to have buried there—perhaps a dear friend or trusted and valued servant.

In most cases you can expect to find forebears buried in cemeteries located in or near the cities and towns they lived in. It is not unusual to find African Americans buried on the outskirts of town in cemeteries set aside for them or in separate sections of a public or church cemetery. Until recently, there was no tombstone or marker in the Whippany cemetery for a single Thompson, although dozens are buried there. Once, when choosing his own burial site in that cemetery, my father remarked quite casually, "We don't do tombstones." Still, he was able to show me, as his father had shown him, where his great-grandparents and grandparents were buried—all, of course, in the "colored" section. My father was also able to recount the circumstances of their deaths and the deaths of a host of lesser relatives. He was a magnificent griot.

My parents will be the last to be buried in the Whippany cemetery, which is now closed to other burials. There is something to be said for living in a town for two hundred years and burying all your kin in the same place. A single marker now identifies the key names from various generations of Thompsons. They rest in close proximity to each other. You may also find that your forebears are buried close to each other in a particular burial ground. Mothers, fathers, sisters, brothers, aunts, and uncles, interred close to each other, can transform a particular piece of cemetery ground into a family plot. Chances are that where you find one forebear, you will discover others. If you know the city in which your ancestors may have been buried, city maps will usually show the location of cemeteries. If a cemetery has been abandoned or closed, you may need to consult historical maps to find the information you need.

Record Keepers

You may find that you have already collected information that tells you where some of your forebears are buried. Death records usually include the burial site and date of burial. Often the funeral director or person in charge of the burial is also identified. If the forebear you are seeking died before death records were routinely kept, you may still discover information about her death by consulting records maintained by the funeral director. Even if the funeral director who handled your family burials has died or gone out of business, his records may be in the possession of the funeral director who currently handles funerals in the town or county where your forebears died.

Sextons' records exist for many public and private cemeteries. These usually include information about who is buried in the graveyard and where each grave is located. It is not unusual for the sexton to oversee a number of tasks: keeping cemetery records, opening and closing graves, and maintaining cemetery grounds. If your ancestors are buried in a cemetery under the care and keeping of a sexton, this sexton can save you time and effort in locating them.

Despite your best efforts, you may find that you are unable to identify burial sites for your forebears. Do not forget about the importance of family oral history. Turn to your family griots for help in finding the cemeteries in which your forebears were laid to rest. Even with their help, your search may not be easy. The information they give you, while correct, may have been altered by circumstances. The burial sites they remember may have been abandoned or poorly maintained. Others may have been covered over for more years than anyone knows.

Abandoned Graveyards

In the summer of 1990 a Dallas, Texas, freeway project was put on hold. Initial excavation had uncovered bodies of hundreds of former slaves and African-American settlers who lay buried in forgotten graves in an area that was now just north of the downtown area. More than a thousand graves were eventually identified. Approximately a year later, in the fall of 1991, before excavations began for a federal office tower in lower Manhattan in New York City, archaeologists uncovered the first of many graves in what was once The Negros [sic] Burial Ground, a colonial cemetery. The burial ground, formerly on the outskirts of the city, once covered nearly six acres and is said to have held the remains of more than ten thousand free and enslaved African Americans who lived and died in Manhattan. As the *New York Times* reported, "It took 200 years for the cemetery used by black New Yorkers in the Colonial era to move from the outskirts of city life to the center of municipal consciousness." Had eighteenth-century African Americans been granted full membership in New York City's churches, they would have been permitted burial in one of the church burial grounds.

Across the continent from New York, just outside Roslyn, Washington, is the African-American Miners' Cemetery, called Mount Olivet. Those buried here were among the first African-American settlers in Washington. Mount Olivet, now a barren hill, is said to have been the burial site for more than two hundred African Americans. Only a dozen or so of the markers that identified their resting places remain.

You can read more about African-American burial sites, both those that have been abandoned and those currently in use, in *Lay Down Body: Living History in African-American Cemeteries* by Roberta Wright and Wilbur Hughes III. The book contains cemetery names and locations that may help you in your search for your forebears. (See bibliography.)

RELYING ON TRANSCRIPTIONS

Cemetery tombstones, especially older ones, can provide a wealth of information. Tombstone inscriptions have included birth and death dates; names of parents, spouses, and children; and information about military service and religious affiliation. There may be circumstances, however, that prevent you from visiting burial grounds and taking advantage of the information to be found on tombstones. Or perhaps you will arrive at a cemetery site only to discover it has been moved, vandalized, or poorly maintained. Gravestones may be overturned or unreadable. In these and other instances, you may find it helpful to turn to transcriptions of the information once easily obtained from tombstones.

During the depression in the 1930s, millions of people were unemployed. In response to this national crisis, President Franklin Roosevelt created the Works Progress Administration, later renamed the Work Projects Administration (WPA), in an attempt to get people back to work. A great variety of jobs was made available, ranging from road building to writing. Some WPA workers copied inscriptions that were found on gravestones in many of this nation's cemeteries. Added to the work done by the WPA is that of various chapters of the Daughters of the American Revolution (DAR), whose members also copied inscriptions from thousands of cemetery tombstones. Other groups interested in genealogy have also copied tombstone inscriptions. Much of this work has been published and placed in libraries in the towns where the cemeteries from which the inscriptions were copied are located. Additional copies of these works are often available in state, regional, and local historical society headquarters.

If you rely on these transcriptions for information about your forebears, some cautions apply. As with all human endeavors, transcribers make mistakes. While the information provided in the transcriptions is better than none, if it is at all possible you will want to verify it. In fairness to the transcribers, it should be noted that tombstone engravers make their fair share of mistakes, too. If you find a birth or death date inscribed on a tombstone that does not jibe with other information you have, do not automatically assume that the tombstone provides the correct information. Instead, flag the discrepancy for further research.

You may wonder if it's really worth your time and effort to go mucking around graveyards. Surely you can find the information you need without having to try to figure out what's written on tombstones, right? Perhaps not. A tombstone may be the only place a foreparent's maiden name exists. A collection of tombstones may be the only indication you have as to the length of time your forebears stayed in a given place. The records of birth, life, family, and death carved on tombstones may be the only such records available to you as you get closer to finding your earliest African-American ancestors. If you are serious about tracing your roots, you will want to take advantage of the information available to you in this nation's burial grounds.

As you work your way back to your earliest African-American ancestors, you are likely to uncover more information about their church affiliations, burial sites, and life activities as recorded on their gravestones. Since you know how valuable this information can be, you know you must be receptive to it wherever and whenever you find it. For the moment, however, you may feel you have exhausted all the church and cemetery records currently available to you. If this is the case, take time to record on your Individual Family Worksheets all the information you have found in churches and cemeteries. This may take some time, because you have probably discovered forebears you did not previously know existed and need to fill out a worksheet for each of them. More than this, you have probably found new information to add to already existing work-sheets. Perhaps a gravestone turned up a great-grandfather's death date or a great-grandmother's birthplace.

Before you continue your research, review your worksheets to make sure you understand the connections between and among the forebears you have learned about. You will also want to bring your genealogical charts up to date so that each of the direct forebears you have information on has a place on these charts. By this time you've figured out that if you record the information you discover in a timely fashion, the task will not become overwhelming.

Once your Individual Family Worksheets and your notes are in good order, file the copies of documents you have found, remembering to keep like documents together. This done, you are ready to tackle one of the most significant sources of genealogical data available to any American tracing roots—federal census data. This data will provide information about your forebears that you may find nowhere else. Moreover, as the government increased its sophistication in data collection, more precise information became available about where people lived, when and where they were born, when and where their parents and their children were born, the time they spent in school, the work they did, the pensions they collected, and even the value of their personal property and the real estate they owned.

The work you have done thus far will permit you to make good use of the data collected by our government. By now you have a good sense of at least some of your forebears. Your research will give you confidence in following the hunches you may have about them—hunches developed, at least in part, by tapping into your family's oral history. You are also ready to discover if the names of towns and people you have heard in your talks with relatives do, in fact, have some meaningful place in your family's history.

The information compiled on your Individual Family Worksheets has provided partial pictures of some of your forebears. At this point you may need only fill in a few more blank spaces to make some of these pictures complete. Federal census data will help you fill in some of these blank spaces. It will also help you discover if your forebears were always free or, if not, when they likely obtained their freedom. Most important, federal census data will provide at least some of the clues you need to trace your roots back to your earliest African-American ancestors.

7

Tackling Federal Census Records

Census records are the nation's gift to the genealogist. A federal census has been conducted every ten years since 1790. A census enumerates, or counts, the population. Still, it is a miracle that the first census ever took place or that there was a nation of Americans to count.

The debate over how the country's population was to be tallied holds special significance for African Americans. In 1787, in the process of adopting a new constitution for the United States, a monumental battle was waged over how states would be represented in the national congress. The most populous states wanted representation in the new government to be determined by population. The smaller states championed equal representation, regardless of size. Adding to the squabble, southern states wanted to count slaves as part of their population when determining representation in Congress but wanted to consider those same slaves as property when determining taxation based on population.

It was only by an ingenious compromise that a constitution was finally adopted. Congress would consist of two branches: a Senate, where all states would be represented equally, and a House of Representatives, where representation would be based on population. A census was to be taken within three years and every subsequent ten years after that to determine the population of the country. When calculating the number of representatives to which they were entitled, southern states were permitted to add to the number of free persons "three fifths of all other persons." Those "other persons" were slaves who just happened to be African Americans. Amazingly, the word *slave* never appears in the U.S. Constitution. Still, according to this document, it took five African-American slaves to equal three free citizens. In return for this concession to the South, the new Constitution specified that the importation of slaves would stop in 1808.

It is of more than passing interest that the framers of the Constitution, who set out to "secure the blessings of liberty to ourselves and our posterity," did not find the courage or the will to abolish slavery in the United States. Although beyond the scope of this book, every American interested in understanding how the slavery issue influenced this nation at its beginnings should read *Miracle at Philadelphia: The Story of the Constitutional Convention May to September 1787* by Catherine Drinker Bowen (see bibliography).

Once the compromise was agreed to, enumerators set out in 1790 to conduct the first national census. These poorly paid public servants went from village to farm to town, gathering information about households and individuals and entering the data they collected on large sheets of paper. These filled-in sheets are called population schedules. You might think that tallying the nation's population would be a simple matter; it was not. Transportation was poor at best, and the people to be counted were often suspicious and sometimes uncooperative. It took enumerators eighteen months to complete the 1790 census, turning in a head count of a little less than four million Americans.

Although this chapter deals with the federal census, a number of state censuses also exist, and these state records may be of some help in locating your forebears—especially if the federal records are missing, as they are in some instances. Most of the state census records are located in the state in which they were taken, either in the state archives or in one of the state historical societies. You will find a listing of state archives and state historical societies in appendix II.

TAKING COUNT

When the first federal census was taken in 1790, there were 757,208 African Americans in the United States. Of these, 59,527 were free and 697,681 were slaves. Approximately 85 percent of these slaves were located in four states: Maryland, Virginia, South Carolina, and North Carolina. Still, every state in the new nation except Maine and Massachusetts had a slave population. When the federal census was taken in 1860, just one year before the start of the Civil War, the slave population in the United States had risen to almost four million (3,953,760), more than a 450 percent increase over the number of slaves in 1790. By 1860 the free African-American population had reached almost half a million (488,070).

In 1870, five years after the Civil War had ended and nearly five years after the ratification of the Thirteenth Amendment to the U.S. Constitution—the amendment that ended slavery in the United States—the African-American population in the country totaled 5,392,172. Somewhere among these more than five million people are forebears of most African Americans living in the United States today.

Even if you know where your foreparents were living at the time of any given census, it will be best to start with the most recent census data available and work your way back—perhaps to 1790, if your forebears were free inhabitants of the United States when the first census was taken. To do otherwise might cause you to miss important information the census data contains, which you may need to find your earliest African-American ancestors. It would be wonderful if you were able to start with the most recent census. This is not possible, however: to protect the privacy of American citizens whose names appear in the population schedules, census data is not released for seventy-two years after it is collected. This means that data collected in 1990, for instance, will not be available to the general public until 2062. The most recent census data available to genealogists as this book goes to press was collected in 1920. Begin your search there.

To many, 1920 does not seem very recent. Do not be discouraged. You are not starting with a blank sheet of paper. You have already collected a great deal of data from your own family records and from the records found in a variety of places, including town halls and courthouses. You may have also gleaned information from church records and cemeteries. Your family's oral history has provided data. All of this information will help you bridge the decades-long gap between the 1920 census and today. In time, you will be amazed at just how recent 1920 is.

KNOWING HOW TO BEGIN:
THE SOUNDEX SYSTEM

Suppose you do not have a clue about where a key ancestor family was living at the time of the 1920 census. You may still be able to find this family using the Soundex Coding System, which is available for the 1880, 1900, and 1920 population schedules. Simply put, the system sorts names according to the way they sound. Letters with similar sounds are given the same code. Although the system may seem complicated at first, it is really quite easy to use.

In addition to indicating the members of a household and their ages, the Soundex file tells you where the family can be found in the census records by listing the district for both the census supervisor and enumerator, along with the sheet number and even line number of the data. The file is arranged first by state; then alphabetically, using the first letter of the surname; and finally numerically, using the Soundex Code. Examples of the Soundex Code include A000, B104, C223, D445. Within each code, the names are listed alphabetically. If several of those listed have the same name, they are listed according to the state or country of their birth. The states and countries are also listed alphabetically.

To use the Soundex Coding System, start with the first letter of the surname you are looking for. (Disregard this letter thereafter.)

Then eliminate all vowels (*a, e, i, o, u*) plus the letters *y, w,* and *h.* Now change the remaining letters to numbers. The chart below tells you how to do this. Your goal is to come up with a three-digit code number. Double letters or two letters with the same code are coded as a single digit. If you do not have enough key letters to make a three-digit code, simply add zeros. If you get a three-digit code before you have used all the letters of the surname, disregard the remaining letters.

SOUNDEX CODING SYSTEM

Code Number	Key Letters
1	b, p, f, v
2	c, s, k, g, j, q, x, z
3	d, t
4	l
5	m, n
6	r

The Soundex code number for some of my own family surnames is as follows:

Name	Letters Coded	Code Number
Anderson	n, d, r	A536
Conover	n, v, r	C516
Thompson	m, p, s	T512
Williams	l, m, s	W452

Perhaps you will discover that the name you need to find has no code numbers—for example, the name *Lee.* (It has no code number because the system requires that you disregard the first letter of the surname and eliminate vowels.) In this particular case, the code for Lee is L000.

Using the Soundex system, you can learn the relationship among various members of a given household. Cross-references help you find related households. When using the Soundex files, remember what you know about the spelling of names. The same name may be spelled in a variety of ways. If you are unable to find a name where you think it should be, use your imagination to determine how the name might have been spelled. Do not rule out abbreviations. For example, in some records my great-great-grandfather's name is written as *Chas.* rather than *Charles.* Consult other Soundex files until you find the family you are looking for.

When you are working your way back, you will find that for 1910, Soundex is available only for twenty-one states. However, a system similar to Soundex, called Soundmaster, is available for some states; a system called Miracode is available for others. If you need 1910 Soundex-type information, check with your librarian to determine if it exists for the state(s) you are interested in. You or your librarian may have to check with the state archivist or with an archivist at one of the regional branches of the National Archives to find what you are looking for. A listing of the regional branches of the National Archives is located in appendix III.

The original Soundex card file is available on microfilm. You can find copies of the Soundex microfilm in most libraries that have census records. If these census records are not available in your local library, your librarian will be able to tell you where you can find them in your area. Once you have the Soundex code, you can use the Soundex microfilm catalog to locate the microfilm number and the roll number on which you will find the code you are interested in. If your library or research center does not have such a catalog, ask if one can be borrowed for you.

SCROLLING THROUGH INFORMATION

Perhaps you already know where your forebears were in 1920. If your parents or grandparents live in the county you inhabit now, you will most likely be able to find 1920 census data you need in your local or county library. In addition to having the area census data on microfilm, your library is also likely to own an index for each census that lists, in alphabetical order, the person or people found in the records for a particular year. If the person you are looking for is listed in the census data, then, the index will tell you exactly where to look in this data. The index listing is arranged alphabetically by surname; this is followed by the given name, the county, the page of microfilm on which the name is found, and finally the census division.

If your library does not have an index for the census year you are interested in, ask if one can be borrowed for you on interlibrary loan. If an index is not available, you will have to put yourself in front of a microfilm reader and scroll through the census data until you find the people you are looking for. Although this may take some time, it is not difficult. Census data is arranged by state and county. You simply have to find the county you want, which is usually marked on the microfilm container, insert the appropriate spool into the reader, and scroll your way through the county census data until you come to the right surname. That is what I did when I began my family history research, simply because indexes were not available to me.

Remember, as an African American you have some help in your scrolling journey: Racial designations, those *B*s, *C*s, and *M*s, stand ready to assist you. In fact, your search will be easier if you first try to locate those of your forebears who were "black," "colored," or "mulatto." For the 1850 census, enumerators were instructed as follows: "In cases where the person is white, leave the space blank. In all cases where the person is black, insert the letter B. If mulatto, insert M. It is very desirable that these particulars be carefully regarded." It seems that these particulars were carefully regarded for not only the 1850 census but also every one after that. Therefore, the color designations are sometimes startlingly easy to find, especially if your forebears were among a few African Americans living in a particular census area.

Even when African Americans are grouped together in certain

census areas, there will be whole pages of data that you can skip before you have to concentrate on finding your forebears among the African Americans listed. Your search will certainly be easier than it would be if race were not identified for you. Be aware that in some population schedules, the enumerator may have written *N* to stand for Negro rather than *B* for black or *C* for colored.

When looking through the 1920 census data, you will find color specified under the major column heading PERSONAL DESCRIPTION, which stands above separate columns for SEX, COLOR OR RACE, AGE AT LAST BIRTHDAY, and MARITAL STATUS (single, married, widowed, or divorced).

BECOMING FAMILIAR WITH THE DATA

Although you will begin your search with the 1920 census, you should have some understanding of the data collected before that year. Following is an overview for each population schedule, beginning with the 1790 census. As you will notice, more data was gathered each time the census was taken. Although similar information was sought in the years between 1790 and 1840, each census differed to some degree in the questions asked and the information sought.

The 1790 Census

Although the United States was made up of only thirteen states in 1790, the census was taken in an area covering seventeen present-day states. Population schedules exist for Connecticut, Maine, Maryland, Massachusetts, New Hampshire, New York, North Carolina, Pennsylvania, Rhode Island, South Carolina, and Vermont. The population schedules for Delaware, Georgia, Kentucky, New Jersey, Tennessee, and Virginia were burned during the War of 1812. However, the population schedules for Virginia were reconstructed from state enumerations.

FEDERAL CENSUS DAY

1790	First Monday in August
1800	First Monday in August
1810	First Monday in August
1820	First Monday in August
1830	June 1
1840	June 1
1850	June 1
1860	June 1
1870	June 1
1880	June 1
1890	First Monday in June
1900	June 1
1910	April 15
1920	January 1

For each household, the 1790 census shows the name of the head of household, the number of free white males under sixteen, the number of free white males sixteen or older, the number of free white females, the number of all other free people, and the number of slaves.

If your forebears were free in 1790, and if the records for the state(s) in which they lived were not destroyed, you should find the head of the household of your family listed in this census. Surnames were not always used to identify free African-American heads of households. Sometimes only a first name is given; at other times only race and number in the household are provided. There are times, however, when the census taker listed the surnames of free African-American heads of households. If you know the surname of a forebear who was free and know where she lived, you may be able to find her in the 1790 data. You will also learn something about the size of the household she headed.

If an ancestor was a slave, the name of the slave owner may be part of your family's oral history. If you know the state in which the slave owner lived, you may be able to find him listed in the 1790 census along with the number of slaves he owned. The data will also tell you the county the owner lived in. This information—the slave owner's name and the state and county in which he lived— may lead you to one of the plantations that was home to your forebears. You will not learn much more from the census data, however. No slave names are included in the 1790 population schedules.

The 1800 Census
Population schedules from the 1800 census exist for fourteen states and are arranged alphabetically by state or territory, county, and sometimes even by town or village. As with the previous census, each entry shows the name of the head of household and the number of free white males and females. For the 1800 census, however, the age categories have been increased beyond those designated in 1790. Those categories are under 10, 10 and under 16, 16 and under 26, 26 and under 45, and older. The age categories for this census apply to both free white males and free white females. All other free people, except Native Americans not taxed (those living on reservations), continue to be numbered only and are not put into age categories. In the population schedules, Native Americans are called Indians. The 1800 census also counted the number of slaves in the population. African Americans can glean the same kind of data from this census as from the 1790.

The 1810 Census
Population schedules from the 1810 census exist for sixteen states and territories. Again, the schedules are arranged by state or territory, county, and sometimes down to town and village. The name of the head of each household continues to be listed. Since slaves were manumitted, or freed, with some degree of regularity, continue to look for your forebears among those listed as free heads of households.

A new age category was added for this census, namely forty-five and older. Again, only free white males and free white females were entered into one of the age categories. All other free people, except Native Americans living on reservations, were simply counted and their number entered into the records.

Information about manufacturing in the United States was also collected in 1810. Except for fragments found among the population schedules, these manufacturing schedules no longer exist. The fragments that remain, however, list the name of the manufacturing business, the owner's name, the kind of business it was, the quantity of goods produced, and the value of those goods. You may find it helpful to consult these manufacturing schedules: Some of America's most gifted craftsmen were African Americans, and it would not be surprising if you found a few free African-American entrepreneurs accounted for in the schedules. The archivist in your regional National Archives branch can help you locate additional information about this data.

The 1820 Census

The 1820 census covered twenty-two states and territories and is arranged in the same way as previous census data: by state or territory, county, and sometimes town and village. Again, the only name that mattered to the census taker was that of the head of the household; all who did not head households were simply counted. Remember, sometimes these heads of households were African American.

The 1820 census added another age category: between 16 and 18—a designation used only for free white males. Free white females continued to be counted in the age categories established in the 1810 census: under 10, 10 and under 16, 16 and under 26, 26 and under 45, 45 and older.

The 1820 census paid some heed to the African-American population. For the first time, African Americans were treated in the same way white nonheads of households were treated: They were counted and placed in age categories. For all African Americans, male and female, free and enslaved, these age categories were under 14, 14 and under 26, 26 and under 45, 45 and older. All other people, except Native Americans living on reservations, were simply counted.

If one of your forebears was head of a household in 1820, you can now determine not only the size of the household she headed but also the sex and age of those who inhabited it. This, when added to other information you have gathered, may help you come closer to identifying some of these household members. For the first time, information was sought about aliens in the population and the number of foreigners who had not become naturalized citizens. Information about occupations was also collected. Again, if one of your forebears was head of a household, you may learn for the first time something about her occupation. This may help you verify other information you have collected.

The 1820 census also included questions about articles being manufactured in the country. A variety of information was sought, including the market value of the products, the quantity and cost of raw materials used, the number of people employed, and the wages paid.

The 1830 Census

The 1830 census is arranged in the same way as previous census data. For the first time, however, enumerators used printed forms of uniform size. Each entry covers two pages. The left-hand side contains primarily family data, and the right-hand side contains slave data.

As should be expected, new information was sought. This time the enumerators were to count the number of people, including slaves, who were blind or deaf-mute. And as should be expected, new age categories were added for free white males and females: under 5, 5 and under 10, 10 and under 15, 15 and under 20, 20 and under 30, 30 and under 40, 40 and under 50, 50 and under 60, 60 and under 70, 70 and under 80, 80 and under 90, 90 and under 100, 100 and older. Free "colored" males and females, along with slaves both male and female, were counted and placed in these age categories: under 10, 10 and under 24, 24 and under 36, 36 and under 55, 55 and under 100, and 100 and older.

The 1840 Census

The 1840 census covered thirty states and territories and is arranged by state or territory, then by county. For this census minor subdivisions were generally used, among them: town, township, parish, precinct, city, ward, and district. As with the 1830 census, enumerators used printed forms. One page continued to contain family information, but the second was designed to gather data on slaves, employment, and pensions. No new age categories were added to those found in the 1830 census.

In its continuing quest to learn more about the population, the government wanted its enumerators to gather information about education, literacy, and military pensioners. Therefore, as instructed, enumerators counted students, the number of free white people older than twenty who could not read and write, and those who were deaf, mute, and blind—both white and "colored." They were also asked to tally the number of people in each family engaged in certain occupations, among them agriculture, manufactures and trade, engineering, mining, commerce, navigation, and learned professions.

Pay careful attention to the fact that enumerators were asked to list the names and ages of those collecting military pensions. If any of your forebears were Revolutionary War combatants or fought in the War of 1812, it is possible that their names are listed among those who collected military pensions. If this is the case, you are likely to discover more about them in military records, which I will discuss in the next chapter.

The 1850 Census

Hang on to your hats—African Americans, at least those who were free inhabitants of the United States, are about to introduce themselves! For the first time we are to learn their names, ages, occupations, and birthplaces. No longer just numbers or just numbers within a certain age group, but people—honest-to-goodness, here-we-are-in-the-flesh, African-American people.

For the first time in federal census-taking history, the name of each free person in a household is given. As if that were not gift enough, the age, sex, color (white, black, mulatto), occupation (for males over fifteen), and value of real estate owned are also shown. Adding icing to an already rich cake, census enumerators were also asked to find out the state, territory, or county of birth for each free person listed. In addition, they were to ascertain if those over twenty could read and write. Finally, the enumerator was to determine if a member of the household was a deaf-mute, blind, insane, an idiot, a pauper, or a convict. How insanity or idiocy was actually determined remains a mystery.

The 1850 population schedules are arranged by state or territory. The status of the state or territory—slave or free—is designated. After this, county and minor subdivisions (city, town, and district, for example) are given. The 1850 schedules for free inhabitants were separated from slave schedules for states where slavery was still protected by law. Slave schedules included the name of the slave owner along with the number of slaves owned and the number that had been manumitted, or freed. Although not named, each slave was listed separately, along with age, color, and sex. In addition, enumerators also recorded whether the slave was a deaf-mute, blind, insane, or idiotic. Finally, the enumerator was to find out if the slave in question was a fugitive from the state.

In addition to the population schedules, the 1850 census data includes mortality, agriculture, and industrial schedules. For the African-American genealogist, the mortality schedules are especially important. They include information for each person who died during the year ending June 1, 1850 (designated census day), including the name, age, sex, color, marital status, place of birth, and occupation. This information may help you find a forebear whose death might, under other circumstances, have caused him to have been overlooked. Because the month of death is also given, you may be able to zero in on birth-date information that was previously unavailable to you.

The 1860 Census

As in the 1850 census, each free person in a household is listed by name, age, sex, color, value of real estate owned, birthplace, whether married during the year, and whether a deaf-mute, blind, insane, an idiot, a pauper, or a convict. For the first time information about the value of personal property was sought. My great-great-grandfather Charles Thompson told the census taker that his real estate was valued at one hundred dollars, and his personal property was worth fifty dollars. I've always wondered what that personal property was.

Like the previous census, the 1860 census includes mortality, agriculture, and industrial schedules. The agriculture schedules, for the year ending June 1, 1860, show the name of the owner, agent, or tenant of farms with an annual produce valued at one hundred dollars or more. They also include information about the land, machinery used, and livestock. If any of your forebears were free and successful owners of thriving farms, you may find more information about their enterprises in the 1860 agricultural schedules.

The 1860 census may yield some unexpected information if your forebears happened to live to a ripe old age. The slave schedules for this census record the name, age, and sometimes the birthplace of slaves over a hundred years of age. The slave owner's name is also given. While only a small number of slaves are identified in this way, probably less than a thousand, if your forebear is among them you may discover an unexpected bonus: the identification of her birthplace. Since she had to have been born no later than 1760 to be included in this data, you may have found, if not your earliest, at least one of your earliest African-American ancestors. She may well have arrived in this country before the British colonies in North America won their freedom from Great Britain.

The 1870 Census

Amendments to the U.S. Constitution stand as witness to the drastic change in the status of African Americans between the 1860 census and the 1870. First, the Thirteenth Amendment, ratified on December 6, 1865, abolished slavery in the United States. Next, the Fourteenth Amendment, ratified on July 9, 1868, conferred citizenship on former slaves who were born or naturalized in the U.S. Finally, the Fifteenth Amendment, ratified on February 3, 1870, approximately four months before the official 1870 census day, mandated that the right of citizens to vote could not be denied or abridged "on account of race, color or previous condition of servitude." On paper, the trip from slavery to full citizenship took just ten years to complete. In fact, the actual journey required more than a century.

The 1870 census was the first conducted after the Civil War and the end of slavery. Therefore, if your ancestors were at home when the census taker arrived, you will be able to find them, even if they had previously been slaves. With the help of this census, the playing field for African-American genealogists and genealogists of other ethnic groups begins to be leveled. From this point forward, everyone has a surname; everyone is to be entered into the census data by this surname and by a number of other identifying characteristics. Now, with fortitude and patience, you have a chance of finding your forebears among the free inhabitants of the United States. Even if you can go back no farther than the 1870 census, this gives you roots more than a century deep in the American soil. Many Americans, even those whose families were not encumbered by slavery, cannot do as well.

Because the data collected for the 1870 population schedules includes the birthplace of parents, you may find some powerful help in locating your earliest African-American ancestors. If the forebear listed in the census data is old enough, he may have reported that his parents were born in Africa and identified the specific country or part thereof. This birthplace information may unlock the last door standing between you and the African forebear who established your family in this country.

For every person who lived in a given household as of June 1, 1870, the 1870 census data includes age; sex; color (white, black, mulatto, Chinese, Native American); profession, occupation, or trade; value of real estate owned; value of personal property; place of birth, including country, if foreign born; birthplace of parents, including country, if foreign born; whether any member of the household was married or attended school within the year; whether each member of the household could read and write; whether any member of the household was deaf and dumb, blind, insane, or idiotic; whether male members of the household were twenty-one years of age or older; and whether any male citizen of the household twenty-one years of age or older had had his right to vote denied or abridged.

The 1870 census also includes mortality, agriculture, and industrial data. The mortality schedules may hold important information if you are seeking foreparents who may have been slaves. For each person who died within the year ending June 1, 1870, the schedules give the name, sex, and race (white, black, mulatto, Chinese, Native American), and tell whether parents were foreign born. The data also shows the occupation of the deceased and the month and cause of death.

The 1880 Census

Each page in the 1880 census shows the post office for the people listed on that page. For each urban household, the name of the street and the house number is shown. This information may make it easier for you to find those forebears who moved within or to specific urban areas. Although African-American migration from the South had not yet reached its peak, this urban data may help you find those who moved from plantation or farm to cities within the South as well as those early migrators to the North and West.

The 1880 census contains data about age, sex, race, birthplaces, and occupations comparable with that collected in 1870. The enumerators were also charged to collect information about how each person in the household was related to the head of the household. Again, this information will be especially valuable to the African American sorting out family ties. Now, if you are lucky and if she told the truth when talking to the census taker, you can discover whether Great-Aunt Lucy who lived with your grandfather really was his sister. The 1880 census data may introduce you to kinfolk you never knew existed.

The 1885 Census

The federal government subsidized, at least in part, a special census taken in five states and territories in 1885. States participating in this census were Colorado, Florida, Nebraska, the Dakota territory, and the New Mexico territory. Mortality schedules are included. The data from this census is available in the National Archives, although not all of it has been microfilmed.

The 1890 Census
A fire in the nation's capital in 1921 destroyed or severely damaged the original 1890 population schedules; less than 1 percent of these schedules remain. A few rolls of microfilm and a few fragments for a few states exist. There is some remaining data from the 1890 census, however, that may be helpful to you. In addition to the regular population schedule, a special census was taken that year for Union soldiers. These records were only partially destroyed. Data for states and territories from Alabama through Kansas and part of Kentucky is missing, but the rest of the information still exists. Included among this data is each soldier's rank, company, regiment, discharge date, length of service, and post office address. Since African Americans served in the Union army during the Civil War, you may find among the data that remains some information about a forebear who was involved in this conflict. This data is on microfilm and available in the National Archives regional centers. You may wish to check with your regional archives branch to see if other remaining data from the 1890 census might be helpful to you.

The 1900 Census
The arrangement of the 1900 population schedules seems to have had the genealogist in mind: They are arranged by state or territory, then by county, and then by minor subdivision (town, city, and ward, for example). Each state is divided into supervisors' districts and enumeration districts. For each household, an entry shows the name of the township, city, and ward, if any, and the street and house number, if in an urban area.

Each person in the household is listed along with relationship to the head of the household, color and sex, month and year of birth, age at last birthday, and marital status. For married women, the data shows the number of children borne and the number of those children still living. Enumerators were asked to record the state, territory, or country of parents' birth for each member of the household. Mindful of the great influx of immigrants from abroad, the 1900 census takers sought information about aliens and naturalized citizens.

Information about the occupation of each person ten years old or older and the number of months not employed was sought. Enumerators also queried householders about school attendance, literacy, and ability to speak English; they attempted to determine whether the residence was a farm and whether the occupant was a homeowner. The 1900 census includes separate schedules for military personnel, including those at U.S. bases overseas and on naval vessels.

A microfilm copy of a card index exists, showing all heads of households in the 1900 schedules, with cross-reference cards for people in the household whose surname is different from that of the head. The cards provide the name, age, and birthplace of each member of the household. They are arranged by state or territory and thereunder by the Soundex system, which I described previously (see page 130). Additional information about this card index can be obtained at your regional National Archives branch.

The 1910 Census
In addition to seeking information about age, color, sex, and marital status, the 1910 census also sought specific information about employment. Individuals were asked to identify the particular industries in which they were employed, whether they were out of work on April 15, 1910, and the number of weeks out of work in 1909. Individuals were also asked if they had attended school at any time since September 1, 1909, and whether they could read any language at all. Information was sought about whether the house being lived in was owned or rented and whether it was mortgage-free. The enumerator was also to learn whether any member of the household was a survivor of the Union or Confederate army or navy. You should not be surprised to find that some of the survivors of the Union or Confederate army or navy were

African Americans, who served in both forces. Finding a forebear listed in the 1910 census as a Civil War survivor may lead you to other information that will help you verify some of the family data you have already collected. You will find more information about tracking military service in the next chapter.

The 1920 Census

The 1920 census names every person living in a household, in addition to identifying street addresses and house numbers. Relationship to the head of the household is also shown. As would be expected, enumerators gathered information on sex, color, race, age, and marital status. Citizenship questions were asked of those not born in the United States; questions about school attendance, literacy, and the ability to write were also asked. Enumerators were also to learn whether a house was owned, rented, and mortgage-free. These home-ownership questions may help you establish your family's accomplishments and aid you in identifying a family home place.

Birth information was sought for each member of a household, to determine whether an individual was born in or outside of the United States. Information about occupation was also sought, and for the 1920 census the enumerator was asked to find out if an individual was an employer, a salary or wage worker, or "working on own account." The answers to these employment questions may help you ferret out early entrepreneurs in your family.

APPLYING CENSUS DATA

Do not expect to get through all the available census data quickly. In fact, some genealogists spend years going thorough the information that exists. You may, of course, stop at any time. Many do, needing a break from the hard work entailed in tracing their roots. Others set aside a day or two a month to continue work that is always fascinating, sometimes frustrating, but, in the end, usually rewarding. Even if you decide to take a break after looking through the 1920 census data, you should do something with the information you have collected from this census. One of the first things you will want to do is to add any new information you find to your Individual Family Worksheets.

The 1920 census data tells you the local community, county, and state in which the data was collected. Did you already have this information? It also includes a complete address for each household—the street and house number. Then it lists every person in a particular household, along with relationship to the head of this household, age, and marital status. Did you find relatives you didn't know existed? Does the data give you new birth information or verify birth information you have already acquired elsewhere? What about the birthplaces of the parents for those listed? Is this information new to you?

Let's assume that you found your great-grandparents listed in the 1920 census. Before looking at the 1920 census data, did you know when your great-grandparents were born or where? Did you know what your great-grandfather's occupation was? Did you know where your great-grandmother's parents (your great-great-grandparents) were born? Did you know whether your great-grandparents could read or write? All of this information is available to you in the 1920 census data. Record it, where appropriate, on your Individual Family Worksheets.

Pay particular attention to birthplaces, which can identify family home places for you and point you in the right direction as you work your way back through census data. When you have gone back through several decades of censuses, you may find it worth your while to visit one or more of these home places—where you may well find records in courthouses, town halls, and historical centers that will help you unlock doors to your family's past. Your forebears may have moved many times since the first census was taken in 1790. Census data will help you track their migration and point to areas of the country that may warrant research or exploration.

Whether they were slaves or free, census data can help you find your way back to your earliest African-American ancestors. Combined with other data and with the records available in your own family, census data helps clear away some of the mysteries of your family's past.

RECOGNIZING THE PROBLEMS

As with much of the data genealogists must use, census records are not perfect. Those questioned were not always forthcoming in their responses. Even when citizens were perfectly honest, the enumerator did not always record their responses correctly. Perhaps he misunderstood what he heard. If you consider the lack of sophistication in early data collection and the opportunities to conceal the truth, you may begin to have doubts about the reliability of *any* census data. Moreover, in the early years it was not unusual for records to be recopied as many as three times. One copy was sent to the federal government for national tabulation, another to the state government, and a third to the county government. The possibility of error occurred each time the records were copied.

Even if your forebears were free inhabitants of this country for all the years census data was collected, you may not find them in every population schedule. Data for the part of the state they lived in may be missing. Despite the fact that they were at home on census day, the enumerator may have missed them, through neglect, laziness, or some other cause. Perhaps, in the enumerator's opinion, your forebears lived in an area too remote to warrant a visit. The way early data was recorded—by hand, using pen and ink—made it possible for your forebears' names to have been obliterated by something as simple as ink blobs.

Sometimes I have found discrepancies when comparing data from one census year with that from another. The 1850 census may say that a forebear was born in 1820. The 1860 census may give the birth date as 1822. And the 1870 census may say she was born in 1824. What gives? First, it is quite possible that the enumerator determined her age from her response to the question on what year she was born, and simply made a mistake in calculation. Perhaps a different person provided the birth-date information each time the census was taken. It could be that the person providing the information made a mistake and was too embarrassed to correct it in front of a stranger.

Nevertheless, you are likely to find your forebears listed in some of the population schedules that are available for your review. Perhaps you will never come up with the exact birth date, for example, for a given forebear. Still, the census records will put you in the right ballpark. That's not bad. Remember, when you are not sure of a birth date—or any other vital statistic, for that matter—flag it on your Individual Family Worksheets as a reminder that you need to do further research. Remember, too, that census data is just part of the information you will use. Information from the family Bible; from birth, marriage, death, or church records; and even from newspaper accounts will help you verify, or perhaps disregard, information you find in the population schedules.

The 1850 records told me that my great-great-great-grandmother Hannah Oakes Conover was thirty-three years old when the census was taken. This would mean that she was born about 1817. By the time I got to the 1880 census, however, her age was given not as sixty-three, but as fifty-nine. If this information is to be believed, she would have been born in 1821. To add more confusion to the issue, the Conover family Bible records Hannah's birthday as Christmas Day, 1828. If that notation is correct, and I suspect it is, Hannah would have been twenty-two, not thirty-three, at the time of the 1850 census.

In the final analysis, I had to ask myself if it really mattered whether my great-great-great-grandmother was born in 1817, 1821, or 1828. And I realized that it didn't matter at all. Over time, I've learned more about her than I ever expected to know. Through research and a collection of family documents, I know when she married; I know the names, birth dates, and many of the death dates of the children she bore; I even have a notice of her death from the local paper. Perhaps someday I will learn when she was actually born. I keep a question mark after her birth date against that day. Until then, and even after, I will delight in her existence. I will continue to be proud of the fact that when the census taker called at the

Conover home in 1850, my great-great-great-grandparents received him and answered, as best they could or as they thought best, his questions.

I am not suggesting that you settle for information that is imprecise. I know from experience, however, that actual dates and other specific pieces of evidence are sometimes hard to come by. Despite your best efforts, you may not be able to nail down a precise birth date or death date. Do not let the lack of precision in this activity discourage you from the task of discovering as much about your African-American ancestors as you can. Delight in every Individual Family Worksheet you are able to complete. Embrace every bit of information that takes you closer to your forebears. Federal census records, despite their shortcomings, provide some of this information and facilitate your journey back toward your earliest African-American ancestors. I am grateful for these records.

8

Using Other Federal
and State Records

In addition to the federal census records, the National
Archives hold a wealth of information useful to you as an
African-American genealogist. Helpful genealogical data is
also found in the nation's Library of Congress. Some of the information available in these resource centers can be accessed via computer. As I discussed in chapter 2, even if you do not own a
computer or do not have access to the Internet, you can still tap
into these databases by taking advantage of computer facilities in
your local or county library. Of course, if you are visiting the
nation's capital, you will want to spend some time at both the
National Archives and the Library of Congress. Finding information
about your forebears among these impressive collections is an exciting experience.

To make effective use of the information housed in the National
Archives, Library of Congress, and any of the state-level research

centers, you will need to know the surnames of the forebears you are seeking. This requirement probably seems less daunting now than it did when you first began to look for your African-American ancestors. By this time, owing primarily to your hard work and diligence, you know and have verified at least some of your ancestors' surnames. You can begin your search through federal and state records using the surnames you know. As you continue to find your way back toward those forebears who established your family in this country, the surnames you know now will lead you to others.

FINDING INFORMATION IN THE NATIONAL ARCHIVES

You will not find a separate collection of materials for African Americans in the National Archives. Rather, you will find information relating to African Americans interspersed among various documents. Moreover, race is not indicated in most archival records. Much of the help you have become accustomed to—provided by those *B*s, *C*s, and *M*s (blacks, coloreds, and mulattoes)—will not exist in many cases. Take heart. The lack of racial designations simply means that, as an African-American genealogist, you now must face the same problems other genealogists face. You will have to dig through existing data to find your forebears, surname in one hand, fortitude in the other, and hope in every fiber of your being. Don't discount hope. Your research thus far has demonstrated that even the hardest work sometimes yields little. As you look through archival records, you will appreciate, perhaps as never before, the times you do find racial designations to facilitate your search.

Some of the archival records that deal with African Americans, while interesting, are not especially helpful to you as a genealogist. Focus on those materials that pertain to individual African Americans rather than to African Americans as a group. Staying focused will not be easy, though: The history of African Americans in the

United States is fascinating. For example, you may find yourself getting caught up in the work of the American Colonization Society, most active in the mid–nineteenth century, whose members financed the transportation of an estimated twelve thousand free African Americans back to Africa. Records pertaining to the work of the society are available in the National Archives. Or you may become intrigued by the westward migration of African Americans in the late nineteenth century, perhaps because you always believed that African Americans moved from South to North. Information about former slaves establishing towns in Oklahoma and Kansas or migrating to California and Washington may be too compelling to resist.

There is no reason not to step away from your genealogy research, from time to time, to explore some of the historical materials that appeal to you and are available among National Archives holdings. But do get back to the business at hand. The work of finding and learning about your African-American ancestors can fill a lifetime. Exploring and understanding African-American history can also fill a lifetime. You will, as a matter of course, uncover some of this history during your search for your roots. Perhaps this will be history enough to satisfy you—this and the sure knowledge that the work you are doing to find your forebears will serve as a legacy for generations of your family to come.

Military Records

Every document in the National Archives, including military documents, has been assigned to a record group, and each record group has a number. In general, a record group contains records of a particular government bureau or, in some cases, an entire agency. A research room attendant at the National Archives in Washington, D.C., or in one of the regional branches will be able to help you find the record group you need.

The National Archives contain information on the wars this nation has been involved in. African Americans fought in all of them, so you will find information in these military records. The sections that follow are only a sampling of the data in the National Archives that pertains to army personnel.

The archives also contain records of those who served in the navy, marine corps, and coast guard. In general, records of enlistees in the navy cover the years from 1798 (when the navy was created) through 1956. Muster and payrolls of ships through 1859 are in Record Group 45. Records for the years 1860 through 1900 are in Record Group 24, *Records of the Bureau of Naval Personnel.*

Record Group 127 contains many of the records of the U.S. Marine Corps, also created in 1798. Records for the U.S. Coast Guard, established in 1915, are found in Record Group 26. Most records for the period after 1895 are located at the National Personnel Records Center in St. Louis, Missouri. If your forebears served in the navy, marine corps, or Coast Guard, do not hesitate to ask for help in finding the records that may contain information about them.

Pension records.   If you are not sure of the conflict(s) in which your African-American ancestors took part, the pension records maintained at the National Archives may help you find out. The data available covers the period from 1775 to 1916 but does not include information about those who served the Confederacy during the Civil War (1861 to 1865). For veterans, pension-record data includes name, rank, military unit, period of service, residence, birthplace, and age. If a widow applied for the pension of a deceased spouse, she was required to provide her maiden name (an important piece of information for the genealogist who has not been able to find this elsewhere) and her husband's death date and place (more valuable information). If children applied for their deceased father's pension, they provided the usual personal information but also gave the dates and places of their births, and the date of their mother's death. Thus you can understand the importance of pension records. Most pension records are in Record Group 15, *Records of the Veterans Administration.*

AMERICAN WARS IN WHICH AFRICAN AMERICANS PARTICIPATED

Conflict	*Dates*
The Revolutionary War	1776–1781
The War of 1812	1812–1814
Indian Wars	1815–1858
Mexican War	1846–1848
Civil War	1861–1865
Spanish-American War	1898
World War I	1917*–1918
World War II	1941*–1945
Korean Conflict	1950–1953
Vietnam Conflict	1961–1973

*Indicates America's entry into the war

The War for Independence. Information about African-American combatants in the Revolutionary War is included in the *List of Black Servicemen Compiled From the War Department Collection of Revolutionary War Records, Special List 36,* compiled by Debra L. Newman. Pension application files also exist and are found in *Revolutionary War Pension and Bounty Land Warrant Application Files,* M804. Selections from the files are found on M805. (*M* and *T* designations indicate the microfilm on which data is found.)

After their defeat, the British left New York in 1783. Many slaves left with them. Lists of these slaves, called Inspection Rolls, were created so that their former owners could be compensated for their loss of property. Consequently, very accurate information was recorded about each slave who left with the British. This includes the name, the sex, a brief physical description of the slave, and the name and residence of the former slave owner. If any of your forebears absconded with the British, leaving the slave owner high and dry, you may able to find them listed on roll 7 of *Miscellaneous*

Papers of the Continental Congress, 1774-1789, M332, and roll 66 of the *Papers of the Continental Congress, 1774-1779*, M247.

The War of 1812. Many of those who fought against the British in the War of 1812 served for less than one year. Most of the National Archives records are arranged by either state or territory, and then by unit. The surname of each soldier is listed alphabetically under his unit. This name index is called *Index to Compiled Service Records of Volunteer Soldiers Who Served During the War of 1812*, M602. The National Archives also contain separate indexes for those who served in units from particular states or territories, and for those who served in miscellaneous units.

Indian Wars. In the forty years following the War of 1812, military personnel were involved in quashing a number of skirmishes called Indian uprisings. Although most who served in these conflicts were free citizens of the United States, Native Americans (originally referred to as American Indians or just plain Indians) also assisted the U.S. government in putting down these hostilities. Records were not kept for every soldier who served in these conflicts, but those that were kept can be found in the *Index to Compiled Service Records of Volunteer Soldiers Who Served During Indian Wars and Disturbances, 1815-1858*, M629.

If records were kept for a forebear of yours who fought in an Indian conflict, the microfilm for this conflict will have a card showing his name, rank, and regiment. This information will be especially helpful if you know your ancestor fought in an Indian War but do not know the specific war he fought in. Between 1815 and 1858 there were at least ten conflicts with Native Americans.

The Mexican War. Many of those who volunteered to fight in the Mexican War (1846 to 1848) had fought in the Indian conflicts and would fight again in the Civil War. The Mexican War drew combatants from twenty-four states, California (which was not yet a state), and the District of Columbia. If your forebears participated in this conflict and you know their surnames, you will find them listed in the *Index to Compiled Service Records of Volunteer Soldiers Who Served During the Mexican War*, M616.

The Civil War.   During the War Between the States, African Americans served with Union forces in regiments of U.S. Colored Troops, and also in the navy and marine corps. You can find information about those who participated in the Civil War in Record Group 94, which is arranged according to military branch. An alphabetical index also exists: *Index to Compiled Service Records of Volunteer Union Soldiers Who Served With the United States Colored Troops,* M589.

The Colored Troops Division of the Adjutant General's Office was responsible for recruiting African-American soldiers. Division records dated 1863 to 1889, are part of the *Records of the Adjutant General's Office, 1780s–1917,* Record Group 94. This record group contains files pertaining to individual African-American soldiers. Colored Troops Division records also include fifty-four volumes listing African-American volunteers who enlisted in Missouri in 1864. These lists give each soldier's name, age, eye and hair color, complexion, height, birthplace, occupation, and date of enlistment. Relying on old habits, "black" or "colored" is sometimes written under COMPLEXION.

If the enlistee was a former slave, the former slave owner's name is given. Data about various African-American troop regiments can be found in volume 8 of the *Official Register of the Volunteer Force of the United States Army;* the years you want to consult are 1861 through 1865. Comparable information can also be found in *War of Rebellion, A Compilation of the Official Records of the Union and Confederate Armies,* published by the War Department and available on M262.

African Americans also served the Confederacy during the Civil War but served in otherwise white units. The National Archives has no records that list the race of these combatants. If you know the names of your forebears who fought for the Confederacy, however, you should be able to find them in archival records.

Creation of all-African-American military units.   After the Civil War, African Americans served in the regular army, albeit a segregated one. The Ninth and Tenth U.S. Cavalries and the Thirty-eighth, Thirty-ninth, Fortieth, and Forty-first Infantry Regiments were organized as all-African-American units in July 1866. In 1869 the four infantry units were consolidated to form the Twenty-fourth and Twenty-fifth Regiments.

The Ninth and Tenth U.S. Cavalries were the famed Buffalo Soldiers, who were among those charged with "pacifying" the West. These African-American cavalrymen put down civil disorders, pursued Native Americans who left reservations, protected survey parties, and guarded stagecoaches. They got their name from their adversaries because, it is said, their short curly hair reminded Native Americans of the buffalo, an animal they considered sacred. It was a name given in respect.

One of my relatives, William Thompson, was a member of the Tenth U.S. Cavalry from 1888 to 1893. He was the youngest son of my great-great-grandparents Charles and Anastacia Thompson. When describing his eyes, hair, and complexion, one word was written three times: *black.* From the REMARKS column I discovered that he was discharged at Fort Custer, Montana, in 1893 and that he was a trumpeter for his regiment. A single word followed those remarks: *Excellent.* I don't know if that meant he was an excellent military man or an excellent trumpeter or an excellent something else. The fact that I never will know really doesn't matter. What does matter is that he adds a little luster to our genealogy chart.

I would never have found my family's Buffalo Soldier had it not been for our family's oral history. My great-aunt Elizabeth always referred to him as "the one that went out West to fight in them Indian Wars and brought home that crazy ol' Indian woman." On a visit to the National Archives, I decided to try to find him, just in case. Since I knew when he was born (1864), I knew which conflict he was likely to have fought in. Just as important, I knew his surname. I found him by scrolling through the *Register of Enlistments for the United States Army* for the 1880s.

Thankfully, the lists are arranged alphabetically. There he was. William Thompson—his hometown, his age, his wonderful blackness—recorded by some person who wrote with a clear hand. For me, the discovery was more than exciting; it taught me to cherish family oral history and to welcome the clues it provides, which had led me to this relative. I never found "that crazy ol' Indian woman," however. Aunt Liz told me that a photograph of her was destroyed when the Thompson trunk went up in flames on that fateful August day.

Looking at the chart on page 154, you can see that the "Indian" War William Thompson fought in was not, in truth, an Indian War. But Great-Aunt Liz knew he was doing something with or to those Indians out there in the West. So, to her, it was an Indian War. Or maybe she listened as her uncle regaled the family with tales of his military exploits, couching these tales in warlike terms. Perhaps from his point of view, and therefore from hers, he *was* involved in an Indian War. Certainly, the activities of the Buffalo Soldiers had all the characteristics of war. I point this out simply as a reminder that while you will look for clues in your family's oral history, you must remember that oral history is not always 100 percent accurate. Still, without Great-Aunt Elizabeth's help I would never have known of William Thompson or taken the time to look for him.

Registers of enlistment and muster rolls. Registers of enlistment (the same registers in which I found William Thompson) cover particular periods of time, beginning with 1798 and ending with 1913. In general, those registers covering 1798 to 1821 show a soldier's name, military organization, physical description, birth date, place of birth, and enlistment information. The registers covering 1821 to 1913 show, among other information, the enlistee's name, when and where he enlisted, the period of time for which he enlisted, his place of birth, his age, his civilian occupation, and a personal description. Information about date and place of discharge is also given. To find your military forebears in the registers of enlistment, you must know their surnames and when they served.

A review of muster rolls may also provide some information about your ancestors who served in the military. A muster roll is a list of all troops present or accounted for on the day of muster (review of armed troops). Muster rolls are considered fairly reliable, since this was the information the paymaster used to issue pay. Regular army troops mustered for pay on the last day of February, April, June, August, October, and December.

In addition to names, muster rolls provide other valuable information, including the date and place of enlistment, the enlistment period, the date and amount of last pay, and an identification of the pay period. The rolls also give information about birthplace, the occupation before joining the military, and a physical description. This physical description is as close as you will come to determining the color or race the soldier in question. If you are as lucky as I was, you will find that single word, *black,* under the columns COLOR OF EYES, HAIR, and COMPLEXION. (I don't know if William Thompson had black eyes or if the person recording his physical description wanted to be sure everyone was aware that he was African American.) If you think a review of muster rolls will help you in your search for an African-American forebear, you must know the unit he was assigned to and the dates he served. Then an archivist will be able to assist you in finding the muster rolls you need.

The Spanish-American War and the Philippine Insurrection. The famed Buffalo Soldiers, who gained such notoriety protecting citizens in the West, were also very active in the Spanish-American War. Both the Ninth and Tenth U.S. Cavalries took part in the conflict. African-American army and naval personnel also participated. When the U.S. battleship *Maine* exploded and sank in Havana Harbor on February 15, 1898, 250 men lost their lives. Two African-American sailors were among them.

An index identifies volunteers who fought in the Spanish-American War: the *General Index to Compiled Service Records of Volunteer Soldiers Who Served During the War With Spain,* M871. Each index card gives the name, rank, and unit in which the combatant served. As an additional aid to the genealogist, the index contains cross-references to names that appear in the records under more than one spelling. Similar information exists for those who took part in the Philippine Insurrection. Two indexes may provide useful information about those African Americans who helped quell this insurrection: the *Index to Compiled Service Records of Volunteer Soldiers Who Served During the Philippine Insurrection,* M872, and the *Index to General Correspondence of the Adjutant General's Office, 1890–1917,* M698.

World War I.   World War I draft records are housed at the National Archives Regional Branch in Atlanta and are part of the *Records of the Selective Service (World War I)*, Record Group 163. Draft registration cards provide a wealth of information to the genealogist—information originally provided by the person registering for the draft. Included are name, address, birth date and -place, age, race, occupation, marital status, and father's birthplace. The cards are arranged alphabetically by state, then by local draft board, and then by the name of the person registering.

Post-World War I conflicts.   The National Archives does not house data from twentieth-century wars after World War I; these records are kept at the National Personnel Records Center in St. Louis, Missouri. Some are protected by the Privacy Act of 1974. This act does not apply, however, to military personnel who are deceased. To gain access to such records, the next of kin (widow or widower who has not remarried, son, daughter, father, mother, brother, or sister) must give written consent to have the records released. Sadly, a 1973 fire at the center destroyed the records of many who served in post–World War I conflicts.

Freedmen's Bureau Records

The National Archives maintains Freedmen's Bureau records, an important research resource for African-American genealogists. Officially named the Bureau of Refugees, Freedmen, and Abandoned Lands, the Freedmen's Bureau was created in 1865, after the Civil War, partly to help former slaves make the transition to citizenship. Among the activities undertaken by the Freedmen's Bureau were legalizing marriages that had taken place during slavery, issuing food to destitute former slaves, operating hospitals and camps, and providing transportation to freed slaves who wanted to return to their homes or relocate in other parts of the country. As the Freedmen's Bureau became established, it also helped Union army veterans collect back pay and pensions.

Much of the work undertaken by the Freedmen's Bureau ended in 1869. The bureau itself was abolished in 1872, and its unfinished work turned over to the Freedmen's Branch, Office of the

Adjutant General. Although the records contain useful information for the African-American genealogist—for example, names, residences, occupations, and dates—this information is not easily accessed. To make the best use of the data in the Freedmen's Bureau records, you should be prepared to use much of the family data you have already collected from other sources. You may well have to make a line-by-line search through the available records to find information that will be helpful to you in tracing your roots. The Freedmen's Bureau records are found in Record Group 105 and described in the Records of the Bureau of Refugees, Freedmen, and Abandoned Lands, Washington Headquarters, Preliminary Inventory, 174. Some of these records are on microfilm on rolls M742, M752, and M803.

Marriage records. The Freedmen's Bureau records located in the National Archives include marriage licenses and reports of marriages performed. The reports are arranged alphabetically by state, then alphabetically by the groom's surname. Marriage certificates often include names and residences of both bride and groom, date and location of the marriage, and the name of the person performing the ceremony. In some instances, age, complexion, parents' complexion, and previous marital relationships are included.

Marriage records are far from complete. Moreover, to take advantage of the information these records contain, you must know where your forebears were likely to have been married and the groom's surname. Additional records of marriages are contained in the counties in which the marriages were performed. As I discussed earlier, your visits to county courthouses in your family's home places should uncover some records of family marriages.

Freedmen's Savings and Trust Company. Congress incorporated the Freedmen's Savings and Trust Company primarily for the benefit of former slaves. Although the main office was in Washington, D.C., branch offices were located in a number of cities in Arkansas, Florida, Mississippi, New York, Pennsylvania, Tennessee, and Texas. The branch banks kept registers of depositors, most of whom were African Americans. Although not all the branch offices collected the same information, in the main the information available includes name, age, complexion, birthplace, name of former owner, current residence, occupation, and the names of parents, spouse, children, and siblings. The records also contain depositors' signatures.

The existing registers of depositors are found in the *Records of the Office of the Comptroller of the Currency,* Record Group 101. Microfilm reproductions exist and are identified as *Registers of Signatures of Depositors in Branches of the Freedmen's Savings and Trust Company, 1865–1874,* M816. Although incomplete, register indexes that may be helpful to you also exist: *Indexes to Deposit Ledgers in Branches of the Freedmen's Savings and Trust Company, 1865–1874,* M817.

Other National Archives Records

Among the other records in the National Archives that may help you find your earliest African-American ancestors are some emancipation papers from the years 1862 and 1863 (M433), and some manumission papers from the years 1857 to 1863 (also M433). These documents include information only about those who voluntarily freed their slaves. Some slaves were freed because they had rendered good service to their owners; others paid for their freedom; still others were freed upon the death of their owners.

The National Archives also contain some documents relating to land sold to heads of families between 1863 and 1872. The certificates you may be most interested in are made out to "colored citizens" or "heads of families of the African race." There are also certificates for land leased to African Americans. The records show the name of the buyer and the cost and location of the land purchased. If you believe any of your forebears were land purchasers for the years indicated, one of the archivists or librarians will be able to help you locate this information.

Records of the Bureau of Indian Affairs contain data about those African Americans who sought citizenship in Native American tribes. (Some Native Americans owned African-American slaves.) Gaining citizenship in a tribe was no mean thing. Once citizenship was established, citizens could live on tribal land and share in certain payments awarded these tribes by the U.S. Congress. Claimants were required to present affidavits to prove their right to citizenship. A summary report on this matter, prepared by Commissioner John W. Wallace and called the *Wallace Rolls*, is found in Record Group 75. Much of this material is in the *Final Rolls of Citizens and Freedmen of the Five Civilized Tribes in Indian Territory*, T529.

The National Archives also hold some of the records concerning the sharecropping experiences of African Americans. When slavery ended, many former slaves remained on the plantations they had lived on during slavery and worked as sharecroppers, planting crops and sharing in the harvest. Until the harvest was in, sharecroppers often bought supplies and food at a store owned by the same person who owned the land they farmed. Often, the money they earned from their share of the harvest was consumed by the purchases they had made. As a consequence of their debts, many were as tied to the land as they had been in slavery. If your family was involved in sharecropping, you may find some helpful information in the files of the Colored National Labor Union for the years 1869 to 1874.

Much of the other information contained in the National Archives that deals with the African-American population will not be of specific help to you in tracing your roots, although it may be of interest and help you determine the historical context of your ancestors' experiences in this country. If you are interested in exploring this historical data, an archivist will assist you in finding what you need. Of course, your own research may have encouraged you to explore some archival records. Perhaps you have learned that one of your forebears made a claim to public land while helping settle this country during its westward expansion. Another of your forebears may have been a government employee. Data that applies to land claims and government employment can be found in National Archives holdings. In fact, the list of holdings sometimes seems inexhaustible. Remember, do not hesitate to ask for help to find the information you believe will assist you in your search for your forebears.

When looking for information in the National Archives, try to be aware of reaching the point of diminishing returns. You may find that you are spending hour after hour looking through documents that are not very helpful. Still, some may become useful if you bring more information to the task at hand. This may mean a return to a local courthouse or town hall, or a more thorough review of family documents and oral history. Perhaps you have not yet found some of the key surnames you need. Once you have these names, however, some of the National Archives data may provide other information you need.

Do not worry about having to make repeated trips to the National Archives in Washington, D.C., when you have more information to work with. Regional archives branches are located throughout the United States. You can initiate research in any of these branches in person or by telephone, mail, fax, or E-mail. Regional archives branches are listed in appendix III along with their mailing addresses, telephone numbers, fax numbers, and E-mail addresses.

RECORDS IN THE LIBRARY OF CONGRESS

To help you make good use of the Library of Congress holdings as you search for your African-American forebears, a number of guides have been prepared. Two are: *Afro-American Genealogical Research* and *How to Find Afro-American Sources in the General Reading Room Division.* It would be a good idea to pick up these pamphlets when you arrive at the Library of Congress.

The Library of Congress has a great many publications relating to the African-American experience in the United States. Some of these are of special help to the genealogist. While you can find copies of these publications in other places, perhaps even in your own local library, you may not realize that some of them exist without perusing the Library of Congress holdings. If you have access to a computer and an online service, you can call up the Library of Congress catalog right on your own computer screen. Remember, if you do not own a computer or are not tied in to an online service, you can tap into the Library of Congress catalog and database by using the computer facilities at your local library.

More than four hundred thousand items from the Library of Congress are now available online. According to James Billington, librarian of Congress, the goal is to have five million items online by the year 2000. This massive undertaking, dubbed the National Digital Library, is sure to broaden the library's role as a primary research facility.

Once you begin to become familiar with the materials in the Library of Congress, you may notice listings for a number of family genealogies. You will probably find yourself experiencing a moment of euphoria when you discover one of your family surnames listed among these printed works. Before you assume that that genealogy has anything to do with your family, check your research. Unless you find the same names, along with birthplace and birth and death dates and other salient facts about those you've worked so hard to identify, the printed genealogies you find in the Library of Congress are about someone else's family.

Directories

For the African-American genealogist, the city and county directories found among the Library of Congress holdings may be among the most helpful publications available. County directories usually list owners and operators of businesses and farms. City directories give the name, address, occupation, and employment site for city residents. Many also identify residents by race. The first two city directories appeared in 1785, both for the city of Philadelphia. Although collections of county and city directories exist elsewhere, the Library of Congress has the largest collection by far. Listings in directories are alphabetical by surname and generally include heads of households, adults living in boardinghouses and hotels, and boarders in private homes. The directories were usually compiled by canvassers going from door to door. Anyone not at home was likely to be left out of the upcoming directory, although a neighbor might have provided information.

City directories may help you track your forebears between censuses, as they moved from place to place within a given city. They can also help you locate forebears who may not have been at home to the census taker, or provide information to compensate for missing census data. Some of the earliest directories now exist on microfilm. Although some cities have stopped publishing directories, others continue, and these directories can provide information for at least some of the years for which census records are not yet available for public scrutiny—1930 and beyond. If the directories you are interested in exist, one of the librarians will help you locate them.

Newspapers

Newspapers contain information that may not be available to you elsewhere. It was various issues of a local newspaper that helped me confirm a number of death dates for key family members. Newspapers also helped me confirm addresses and burial sites. The Library of Congress holds an impressive collection of newspapers and newspaper indexes. Some are indexed according to personal name or place. Others index deaths; still others, deaths and marriages.

If no indexes exist for the papers that may contain information about your forebears, it will help if you know the approximate dates for the events you are interested in—deaths and marriages, for example. Even if you know the year of a given death, it may take a long time to find the actual date, because you may have to search through every paper for that year. That means looking through 52 issues if the paper was published weekly, and 365 issues if it was a daily. Moreover, if a forebear died near the end of a year, you may be required to search through that entire year and then into the next, since death notices do not always appear immediately after the death.

I was determined to find my great-grandfather Edward Thompson's death notice. I wanted to see what was written about him at the time of his death. I knew he died in 1913 but I didn't know the day. Of course, I began the search with the January 1913 issues of *The Jerseyman*, the newspaper that served the area he lived in. As luck would have it, Edward Thompson died on December 2, 1913. To get this date, I spent days scrolling through microfilm copies of the paper, enduring its fine print and eight columns per page. As I mentioned earlier, I couldn't focus solely on the obituary column, because until 1937 my forebears' death notices appeared among the news items. When I finally found his death notice, it simply gave his name, his wife's name, the town he lived in, the date of his death, and his burial site—all of which I already knew. When I think about reaching the point of diminishing returns, I think of the effort I expended to find Edward Thompson's death date. You may find that knowing the year a foreparent died is enough for the moment. Your research may be better focused elsewhere.

Slave Narratives

In chapter 6 you read about the work done by the Works Projects Administration (WPA) transcribing tombstone inscriptions and identifying churches attended by African Americans. As you know, these were only two of the many tasks undertaken by the WPA. One of the more exciting undertakings, at least from the African-American genealogist's point of view, was the work done by the Federal Writers' Project. From 1936 to 1939, former slaves were interviewed and their interviews recorded. Interviews were conducted in Alabama, Arizona, Arkansas, Colorado, the District of Columbia, Florida, Georgia, Indiana, Kansas, Kentucky, Maryland, Minnesota, Mississippi, Missouri, Nebraska, New York, North Carolina, Ohio, Oklahoma, Oregon, Rhode Island, South Carolina, Tennessee, Texas, Virginia, and Washington. More than thirty-five hundred former slaves were interviewed for the project, ultimately titled *The American Slave.*

During the interviews for *The American Slave,* former slaves were asked a variety of questions concerning their lives during slavery. The information they shared makes for interesting reading. They talked about their birthplaces, parents, siblings, homes, home life, celebrations, and former owners. If your forebears are among those who were interviewed, you may find a wealth of information that you did not have before.

These interviews were deposited by the Federal Writers' Project in the Library of Congress, where they were assembled under the title *Slave Narratives: A Folk History of Slavery in the United States From Interviews With Former Slaves.* The interviews have also been edited by George Rawick and published in forty-one volumes as *The American Slave: A Composite Autobiography.* You may find copies of these volumes in your local or county library. A number of state archives and historical societies have copies of the interviews with former slaves that were conducted in these states, and some also have the original notes from the interviews.

Because some of the former slaves who were interviewed were no longer living in the state(s) where they had been slaves, you may not find your forebears where you expect. An index for these interviews does exist, however, and lists the slaves interviewed. This index should help you locate the ancestors you are looking for. Unfortunately, the index does not list the relatives or slave owners who are mentioned in the interviews, which would have been helpful to the African-American genealogist. Only a careful reading of the interviews will reveal the names that interviewees spoke about.

As with all resources of this nature, some warnings seem appropriate. You must remember that these interviews with former slaves were conducted more than seventy years after slavery had ended. As a consequence, those interviewed were very old, some ninety years of age. Moreover, these former slaves experienced slavery as children. The combination of old age and childhood memories may not have permitted interviewees to present as accurate a picture of slavery as someone who experienced slavery as an adult might have.

STATE ARCHIVAL AND HISTORICAL SOCIETY RECORDS

In tracing your African-American roots you may find some useful information in state archives and historical societies. These facilities, which exist in every state, maintain records considered important to the history, culture, or government of a particular state and region. Equally important, many families and organizations entrust these establishments with the keeping of their historical documents. Most states are also home to one or more genealogical societies; these, too, maintain records that may be helpful to you.

Although you may decide to visit a particular archive or historical society at some time during your search for your roots, it may be wise to find out something about the holdings of the site beforehand. Appendix II lists the archives and some of the historical and/or genealogical societies located in each state, along with addresses and telephone numbers. You may want to write or telephone the research site you are interested in to request a listing of its holdings. This information may help you determine if a visit would be worthwhile.

Of course, if you plan to be in the town in which an archive or historical society is located, a visit can be instructional and may be helpful. If nothing else, you can introduce yourself to the archivist, librarian, or staff member, inform her of the genealogy work you are doing, and ask if you may keep in touch. Who knows? At some time you may want to place a copy of your own family history in one of the facilities that house information about current or former state residents.

Among the documents in state archives or historical societies are some of the few remaining records of the numerous beneficial societies that were established to help African Americans in the eighteenth and nineteenth centuries. The first of these, the Free African Society, was established in Philadelphia in 1787 by Richard Allen and Absalom Jones. This society and others that followed helped assure that African Americans received assistance when they were sick or infirm, and had burial insurance. Many records of these societies were destroyed. However, if you can find them during your visit to a research facility located in the state where your forebears lived, they may yield valuable information.

Plantation Records

In 1998 bookstores around the country received copies of *Slaves in the Family,* written by Edward Ball, a descendant of South Carolina slave owners. Mr. Ball's family's plantations (they owned several), unlike many others throughout the South, were not destroyed during the Civil War. As a consequence, many of the Ball plantation records, which included deeds, letters, receipts, and lists of slaves, still exist. At the beginning of the twentieth century the Ball family began to entrust family records to archives located in the South, making these documents public records, available to anyone who has an interest in their contents. When writing *Slaves in the Family,* Edward Ball made use of these archival records, including those located in the South Carolina Historical Society, to learn about his family and the slaves it owned.

Mr. Ball also contacted descendants of some of these slaves, who now live in various parts of the country. Perhaps you are among those with whom he met. If so, you know the Ball family plantation records hold information that can be of value as you trace your African-American roots. *Slaves in the Family* also recounts Mr. Ball's identification of a slave named Priscilla, who was sold from Sierra Leone in 1756 and bought by one of his forebears. He tracked Priscilla's descendants to the present day.

Of course, millions of African Americans who were slaves did not work on one of the Ball family's rice plantations. If your forebears are among these millions, you may be able to trace your roots through the records of other plantations. Some of these records, like those of the Balls, have been turned over to state archives or historical societies for safekeeping. You will most likely find plantation records housed in the states that were part of the Confederacy during the Civil War: Alabama, Arkansas, Florida, Georgia, Louisiana, Mississippi, North Carolina, South Carolina, Tennessee, Texas, and Virginia.

To make use of the materials available to you in state research facilities, you must know the state(s) where your forebears were likely to have lived. You may have to rely on your family's oral history for this information. Once you have identified the state, you will also need to know the location of the plantation where your ancestors are likely to have worked. If you know the name of the plantation owner, your search, although not simple, will be easier.

You may well have found that plantation owner's name in your review of the census data that identified slave owners.

Be aware, however, that even if you know the plantation your forebears worked on and the name of its owner, you may not find plantation records in the state where you would expect to locate them. Perhaps the plantation owner's descendants moved and took the records with them, entrusting those records to an archive or historical society in their new home state. It could be that a descendant decided to donate family plantation records to a college or university far from the original plantation site. Or, as is sometimes the case, plantation records may still be in family hands, inaccessible to all except those to whom the family wishes to grant research privileges. Still, if plantation records are available, one of the archivists in the state archives or historical society of the state where the plantation was located will more than likely know of their existence, and may be able to tell you how and where to find them.

Even if you find plantation records that contain the name of one or more of your ancestors, you will usually locate these ancestors identified only by a given name. Again, your family's oral history may provide the information you need to determine if one or more of the slaves listed in the plantation records you unearth is one of your forebears. You may need to review your family oral history notes, paying special attention to given names that are part of your family's collective memory. This information will be crucial in an examination of plantation records. If you can identify one of the slaves listed as one of your forebears, the plantation records may tell you something about this individual that you were unable to find elsewhere: usually a birth date and the name of the mother. Again, the mother of a slave child is usually identified by first name only.

Purchase documents.   The plantation records may also contain bills of sale, telling when and where given slaves were purchased. This information may be among the most valuable you uncover in your search for your African-American forebears. Purchase documents often identify the person who sold the slaves. This person may well have been a shipmaster or agent, whose name and vessel are part of the record. If this is the case, you will know the name of the ship that transported your forebears to this country. You may also be able to identify the African port from which this vessel sailed and the American port at which it arrived. This information may help you find your way back to the African homeland of your foreparents.

Wills.   Remember that slaves were considered valuable property. As such, they were often passed from one generation to another, along with other valuable property. If your forebears were given to other members of a plantation owner's family, you are likely to find this bequest in the owner's will. Wills are often found among other plantation records housed in state archives or historical societies. Frequently, a collection of wills from a given plantation will help you track the transfer of a forebear from one owner to another.

Estate inventories.   Plantation records may also contain estate inventories, which are simply lists that note all the holdings of a given estate or plantation. Among these holdings may well be lists of slaves, identified usually by first name, perhaps by age, and perhaps by the work they did. Again, if you can identify one of these slaves as an ancestor, you may discover information about him that is unavailable elsewhere. Your family oral history can provide a powerful assist in taking advantage of the information found in estate inventories.

Manumission documents.   If your forebears were freed from slavery before the enactment of the Emancipation Proclamation or before the ratification of the Thirteenth Amendment to the Constitution of the United States, they will have been given manumission papers that testify to their freedom. State archives and historical societies have become repositories for some of the remaining manumission documents that are not in private hands. The information these documents contain, indicating when a particular slave or group of slaves was freed, is especially valuable. As you remember, free heads of households are listed in census population schedules. Once your forebear was freed, if you can determine the surname she chose to use, you should be able to find her in the census data. If a forebear was freed before the 1850 census was taken and there-

fore listed in the 1850 population schedule, you may tap into some
of the information you need to take you back to your earliest
African-American ancestors. Remember that the 1850 census
includes not only when a person was born, but also where.

Some manumission documents are located in university libraries.
If your search through state archives and historical society holdings
turns up nothing, you may wish to consult with a librarian at one of
the major universities in your state. Even if this institution does not
have manumission records or information about them, the librarian may well be able to point you in the right direction. When
searching for manumission documents, don't overlook the plantation owner's name or—remembering spelling errors—some variation of it. The documents may be filed under this owner's name,
since it may well be the surname your forebear chose to use.

Church affiliation.   Plantation records sometimes include the
name of the church that the plantation owner's family attended. It
was not unusual for slaves the family owned to worship in the same
place. As a consequence, you may find information about these
slaves—including the church rites they participated in, especially
baptism—noted somewhere in plantation records. If a slave was
baptized, his name and the date the rite was administered will often
be recorded.

Newspapers and Periodicals

State archives and historical societies usually contain a wealth of
publications that relate to the state and region in which the facility
is located. Nineteenth-century newspapers often carried notices of
runaway slaves, which provided the slave owner's name and often
the name and location of the plantation. The notices frequently
included some physical description of the slave to aid in the capture. Not many of us know the physical characteristics of a given
ancestor. However, if some of these characteristics were particularly
distinguishing and memorable, they may well be a part of family
oral history. "The hair on her head was as red as rust." "He got
branded bad. Had three of 'em running right down his back." Such
oral history may fit the description of a runaway printed in a news-

paper. If the description sounds familiar to you, note the name of the plantation contained in the advertisement. If records from this plantation still exist, you may learn more about this daring ancestor and her kin.

Local papers published during the nineteenth century also reported vital statistics: births, marriages, deaths. Unfortunately, many of these papers are not indexed. If, however, you have a fairly good idea when a forebear was born or died, you may want to try your hand at finding verification of these facts in local papers. Scrolling through old newspapers is no easy task. The pages are sometimes large, the type is usually small, and the organization of material is often capricious. In most instances, however, you will find some kind of index to the contents of a given issue, often located at the bottom of the first or second page. This index will tell you where certain vital statistics are found. If you do not find your forebears where you expect to, though, do not give up right away. Information about them may be elsewhere in the periodical you are reviewing. Remember, work only to the point of diminishing returns, not beyond it.

Religious Organizations
Archival and historical society holdings also contain information about religious organizations that were located in the facility's state or region. Sometimes these facilities have been entrusted with original church records that detail membership. Remember that during slavery and even after, African Americans were often members of congregations that were primarily white. Many religious groups or denominations made attempts to "Christianize" the slaves among them. As a consequence, you may find baptismal or other information about one of your forebears among church records.

Church records are not limited to archives and historical societies located in the former Confederate States. To find the church records that are meaningful to you, concentrate on the state(s) in which your forebears lived and check on the holdings in the archives in these states. If you do not find the church records you are looking for, ask the librarian for help. A computer database check may turn up the information you need.

Other Archival and Historical Data

Archives and historical societies have a wealth of other information that may be helpful to you. You may be able to locate information about the burial site of one or more of your forebears by consulting the information the research facility has on cemeteries. Sometimes this includes maps showing where particular people are interred. It is not unusual to find the "segregated" portion of the cemetery designated on the map. If the forebear you are seeking is African American or someone of mixed race, you are likely to find him in this section. You may also find the names of forebears on historical land maps that show the residences of particular families. Among collections of photographs or paintings you may find images of local area residents or buildings that give form and shape to a forebear or to a home place.

If you decide to visit an archive or historical society, plan to stay in the area for several days. It is virtually impossible to check in a single day everything that may be of help. Moreover, information you request may have to be retrieved from another location and not be available until late on the day you request it, or even the next day. Even when the material you request is available right away, it may take you some time to glean from it the information you need. Perhaps a family vacation can be planned around a trip to an archive or historical society. After all, you are likely to be visiting one of your family's home places. Who knows what surprises you will find there?

9

Putting It All Together

In 1624 William Tucker, the first African American born in the British North American colonies, was baptized in the Jamestown settlement in Virginia. Almost four centuries later, in 1998, Thelma Williams, a Virginia resident, reported her continuing thirty-year quest to prove that she is William Tucker's direct descendant. Ms. Williams's determination to validate this centuries-old relationship has been spurred on at least in part by her family's oral history. She reports having first heard of her connection to William Tucker from her grandmother, who passed it on from her own grandparents, who learned it from *their* grandparents. Like so many other African Americans, Thelma Williams has depended on her family's oral history to help her trace her roots. And like so many other African Americans, Ms. Williams has worked hard to find documentation to support this oral history.

Ms. Williams does not know if William Tucker's parents, Anthony and Isabella, were slaves or indentured servants. Nor does she know if they were among the first Africans to arrive at the Jamestown settlement in 1619 on a Dutch man-of-war. She does believe, however, that they are the people mentioned in a

176

1624–1625 census entry that shows the household of Captain William Tucker to include "Antoney Negro and Isabell Negro and William theire child baptised." She also believes Captain Tucker gave William his name, although this fact has not been established. William Tucker's birth record, if it ever existed, has been lost or destroyed.

Ms. Williams does not doubt her kinship with William Tucker. You may envy her confidence. In fact, you may be beginning to wonder just how much more you have to do to find your earliest African-American ancestors. You have already collected a great deal of information about your forebears. You have filled out many Individual Family Worksheets, conducted interviews with family members, gathered together documents that tell how and where your family has lived and worked and saved and spent, perhaps over many generations. You have also constructed a number of genealogical charts that show your connection to those who came before you and their connection to those who came before them.

Your research has doubtless taken you to courthouses and town halls. You have examined available census and military records for information about your ancestors, pored over church records, and visited cemeteries. You have studied directories to follow your family's movements and tracked down newspapers to discover important events in their lives. You have probably contacted personnel at state archives and in historical or genealogical societies to determine if any records were available to assist you in your search for your forebears. Perhaps you have even visited these sites to review plantation records or diaries of slave owners. What now? Now it's time to begin weaving together the separate pieces of your family's story. As you do so, you will develop a greater appreciation for the information you have gathered and a greater understanding of the information you still need.

You may be closer to finding your earliest African-American ancestors than you know. But despite the sometimes overpowering anticipation of finding them, there is no particular schedule you have to adhere to. As you know by now, tracing your roots is a time-demanding, time-consuming activity. Accept this and take your time. Remember, Thelma Williams has been at it for at least thirty years. Others have been searching for their roots even longer.

AN ORAL HISTORY NAME SEARCH

You have gathered a wealth of family oral history. Most of this information is located in the oral history sections of your research notebooks, or wherever else you have chosen to file it. You now want to look through this oral history with a particular purpose in mind. You are going to look for names—those that are most likely to take you back to your earliest African-American ancestors.

Tribal Names

Most Africans who were sold into slavery on the North American continent came from West Africa. Therefore, it is likely that your African ancestors came from one of the nations or tribes of that region. Among the key groups that populated the western part of the African continent are the *Senufo,* found on the west coast; the *Yoruba,* who populate southwestern Nigeria and southeastern and central Benin; the *Guro,* who inhabit areas of the Ivory Coast; the *Ibo,* who are located in the eastern region of Nigeria; and the *Hausa,* who are found in the northwestern region of Nigeria and the eastern section of Niger.

Are any of these tribal names or possible corruptions of them part of your family oral history? Has more than one relative mentioned any of these names? Do your oral history notes contain other names that could be names of African tribes? If so, remember them. You may run across them again as you review other information you have recorded or heard. These tribal names or others may link up directly to particular slaves who may have been your forebears.

At this point, you may want to learn more about African tribes during slavery. If so, you can find any number of works listed in *Books in Print,* published by R. R. Bowker. Your librarian may also suggest materials that may be useful. You might want to consult *Lest We Forget: The Passage From Africa to Slavery and Emancipation* by Velma Maia Thomas, which identifies some of the African tribes from which slaves were taken and shows where they lived on the African continent. The book is easy to read, and its graphics are helpful. (See bibliography.)

Ship Names
When you first recorded names your relatives shared, it may not have occurred to you that some of the them were ship names. In the late eighteenth and early nineteenth centuries, girls' names were popular ship names: Mary Ann, Sally, Diana, and Ruby, for example. A ship name is usually preceded by *the*, as in the *Mary Ann* or the *Diana*. If you have been unable to link names in your notes to people, they may refer to ships. If, on reflection, you think one or two of the names in your oral history notes do, in fact, refer to ships, visit or telephone the relatives who told you of these names and simply ask. (Remember, a visit is sometimes more profitable than a telephone call. Wonderful memories can be triggered by something as simple as sharing a serving of peach cobbler.)

If you can discover the name of a slave ship, other important information may emerge—for example, the name of the port where this ship landed. Obviously, not all slave ships were christened with girls' names. The *Othello,* the *Reformation,* and the *Perseverance* were also among the names that identified slave ships. In fact, there were probably as many slave ship names as there were ship owners to choose them. If upon further discussion a relative cannot substantiate the ship-name theory, try to solicit memories that may uncover information—any information—about your ancestors' journey from Africa to North America.

Port Names
North American ports that received African slaves were Baltimore, Boston, Charleston, Newport, New York, Philadelphia, and Savannah. At various points slave shipments were also received at Annapolis and Cambridge, Maryland; Bristol and New London, Connecticut; Newburyport and Salem, Massachusetts; Providence, Rhode Island; and Roanoke, Virginia. In general, you will be most interested in reviewing those notes that focus on the name of the

port nearest the plantation or workplace your ancestors found themselves in. For example, if some of your ancestors were sold to South Carolina rice planters, the ship carrying them may have docked at Charleston, and they may have been sold at auction near this city.

Do not give up if you cannot find a link between a southern port and a southern plantation, though. Some slave ships that docked in the North—in Boston or Newport, for example—carried cargo that was ultimately sold to southern plantation owners. Perhaps more than one person in your family tells of forebears who landed in Rhode Island. Again, do not ignore family stories because they seem contradictory. The fact that your forebears were purchased by a Virginia tobacco planter does not eliminate the possibility that the ship carrying them to the North American colonies docked at Newport.

Further, in the absence of other proof, do not automatically assume that a forebear was sold to a southern plantation owner. Slavery in the United States was not limited to south of the Mason-Dixon line. In fact, in the 1750s and 1760s Newport, Rhode Island, was the most important slavery zone in the British North American colonies and used more slaves in small businesses, farms, and homes than any other northern colony. Before the American War for Independence, New York was also an important slave port.

Zeroing in on port names that will help you find your earliest African-American ancestors is far from easy. Moreover, the suitability and popularity of slave ports varied as circumstances changed. Any American who engaged in the importation of slaves after 1808, the year when such importation became illegal in the United States, was subject to heavy fines and confiscation of property. These penalties did not, however, succeed in completely curtailing slave traffic in the U.S.

The buying and selling of slaves was an international business for centuries. Despite its complexity, you may find it helpful to learn more about the slave trade and its participants. The librarian in your local public library will be able to help you locate books on the subject. One such work, *The Slave Trade: The Story of the*

Atlantic Slave Trade 1440–1870 by Hugh Thomas, includes slave ship routes, slave ports, points of purchase in Africa, and points of sale in the Caribbean and in North and South America. *The Slave Trade* may contain names of ships, ship captains, or slave ports and harbors that are part of your family oral history (again, see bibliography).

Slave Names

Unfortunately, slave ship manifests did not list their human cargo by name; at best, they identified the number and sex of those on board. Still, those of your African forebears who were sold into slavery did have names, although the names they were given by their purchasers probably bore no resemblance to the names they had when part of their African family groups. Just as important, however, is the fact that many who were sold into slavery maintained their African names among themselves. These names were sometimes known by their descendants.

Perhaps your family's oral history contains one or two names that sound as if they might be African. Yet no two members of your family remember the name the same way or pronounce it in the same way. When you were conducting your initial interviews, you may not have paid too much attention to the names that were being shared. Now it is time to pay attention. You may find it helpful to consult *Names From Africa: Their Origin, Meaning, and Pronunciation*, by Ogonna Chuks-orji (see the bibliography). Review the names included in this slim volume; you may find one that strikes a familiar chord.

If you do, share this name with the relatives who first mentioned it to you. They may agree that this name sounds like the one that was passed down to them from grandparents or great-grandparents. If you find this African name, you are also likely to discover where your African ancestors lived before being sold into slavery. Compare this location with the location of a tribe or clan that may be part of your family's oral tradition. If they match, you may be close to your African roots.

Although your African-American forebears may have maintained their African names among themselves, you cannot ignore the names they were given by slave owners. In bondage, most slaves were identified by a single name. Search your oral history notes for these single names. The ones you will be most interested in are those that have come down through generations of your family. Perhaps your family has even continued to use a particular name for one or two members of each generation. List these single names, along with any characteristics that identified the first in your family to be called by them. Include height, weight, color, deformity, skills, and talents.

Slave Owner and Plantation Names

You have been mindful of slave owner names and plantation names for some time. To make sure you have not overlooked one or two that may be important to you, review your oral history notes just once more to see if your family lore contains stories about living on a particular person's plantation or having been freed by a particular person. Does your oral history include anything about taking a slave owner's surname or discarding it? Are there stories in your family about a slave owner's family that may give you clues to this owner's identity?

Does your family oral history place your earliest ancestors in a particular state? Does the name of a particular county in that state figure prominently in conversation about early ancestors? Is there a strange-sounding name that keeps coming up in discussions about your ancestors, a name that, upon greater reflection, could be the corruption of a plantation name? Do your family memories include descriptions of rivers, towns, or foliage that might help describe the plantation your earliest ancestors lived on?

A Census Records Check

You know that your African-American forebears could have obtained freedom at any time after arriving in this country. Therefore, it will be important to make sure you have not overlooked them in census data. Do not forget about census data collected at the state level. Once you have found your forebears in federal census data, you will know the state in which they were living at the time a given census was taken. Use this information to cross-reference state census data. When looking for free African-American ancestors, remember that your local, county, and state libraries may carry publications based at least in part on census data about free African-American populations in your state. A few such titles are: *Free Blacks in Norfolk, Virginia, 1790–1860: The Darker Side of Freedom* by Tommy L. Bogger; *Freedom's Port: The African-American Community of Baltimore, 1790–1860* by Christopher Phillips; *Makin' Free: African-Americans in the Northwest Territory* by Reginald R. Larry; *Black Slaveowners: Free Black Slave Masters in South Carolina, 1790–1860* by Larry Koger; and *California's Black Pioneers: A Brief Historical Survey* by Kenneth G. Goode. If you have not done so already, check these publications.

As you know, the 1850 federal census was a landmark in census taking, simply because of the wealth of information it contains. If you are able to find an ancestor who was free at the time of this census, you will learn her age and birthplace. If she was fifty years old at the time of the 1850 census, she was born in 1800. The information about birthplace may identify her as the African ancestor you are looking for.

By the time the 1870 census was taken, slavery had been abolished in the United States. In addition to names, the 1870 census data also includes information about birthplaces. The form used to record information about your forebears will tell you the state, the county, the town or township, and even the post office in which data about each forebear was collected. Chances are that in 1870 he was still living in or quite near the place he was born. Does the city or state of his birth have any significance in your family oral history? Perhaps even more important, enumerators were asked to indicate if the parents of the person listed in the population schedule were "foreign born." Certainly, if parents were born in Africa, they would be considered foreign born. Therefore, you will want to review the 1870 census data just to be sure you have not overlooked the very information you were looking for—a direct link back to

Africa. Also, note the birthplace of the person listed in the population schedule; this may tell you where his African parents first lived in this country.

Using the census indexes and starting with the year 1790, search once more for the name(s) your family's oral history tells you belonged to the owner of the plantation your forebears lived on. If you do not find the name where you expect, experiment with other possible spellings. It may take you some time to find the name of a slave owner that seems to ring a bell. The location information at the top of the population schedules will help you narrow your search. Use it. Record every name that might be a possibility. Discuss the likely names with the relatives who shared slave owners' names with you. Review county and state locations to see if this calls up supporting data.

Carrying out this kind of analysis of census data takes time. And effort. And determination. Still, think of the generations it took it for your earliest African-American ancestors to get lost or buried in the pages of American history or of some plantation owner's records.

ARCHIVAL RECORDS REVIEW

Because you looked for and through archival materials, you know how much luck is involved in discovering anything that will help you find your way back to your earliest African-American forebears. Yet every African American profits when another of us accomplishes this feat. When reviewing the information you have gathered from archival holdings, pay particular attention to any wills that may have transferred slaves from one generation to another; manumission records; legal documents that may deal with slave transfers or sales; auctions, where slaves may have been purchased; property inventories, including human property; slave purchases and sales; slave births and deaths; diaries; correspondence; Bible notations; newspaper notices of runaway slaves that may carry names and distinguishing characteristics; records of slave punishments; records of the clothing furnished to slaves.

A careful review of plantation records—and sometimes a second or third review—may uncover the purchase of a slave who bore the same name that your family history points to as old. These records may tell you when and where the slave was purchased. If you know the purchase site, you may be able to determine the name of the port where the ship carrying the slave docked. The name of the port may lead you to the name of a ship. The name of a ship may lead you to an African purchase site.

After purchase, the plantation owner will have recorded the sex and approximate ages of the slaves purchased, the price paid for each, and the name given to each. The slave owner may also have indicated the point of purchase, corroborating information you may already have. Some of this information may connect to information that has been in your family for a long time.

When you are reviewing your notes from archival research, make allowances for mistakes you may have made in transcribing information. As I discussed earlier, handwritten documents are sometimes difficult to decipher. If a name or fact you have transcribed is remarkably similar to a name or fact you found somewhere else, you may want to ask the archivist to send you a copy of the particular page for reexamination. The cost will in all likelihood be minimal, and a review of the original page may make the investment well worthwhile.

THE UNDERGROUND RAILROAD CONNECTION

It has been estimated that between 1830 and 1860, fifty thousand slaves escaped slavery via the Underground Railroad, a secret, ever-changing network of hiding places. More than three thousand men and women were involved in helping these slaves escape. Harriet Tubman, an escaped slave herself, is said to have returned to the South nineteen times after her escape, rescuing three hundred slaves, including members of her own family.

Some who helped slaves escape to freedom along the Underground Railroad kept records of their "passengers." Some of these records, diaries, and personal correspondence are now maintained in libraries, historical societies, and archival centers along the paths that marked this freedom trail. You are most likely to find these records in research centers in Pennsylvania, Connecticut, New York, Vermont, Ohio, and Ontario, Canada. If you know the name of town where a forebear settled after escaping from slavery, check with the archivist or librarian there to find out if the facility is among those that maintains records of the Underground Railroad. If it is, you may find information about the plantation from which your forebear escaped. Once you know this, you may be able to ferret out more information about her life on this plantation, including when she arrived in this country and from where.

In William Still's *The Underground Rail Road,* written in 1872 (see bibliography), you will find scores of actual names (given and surnames) and reports of life in bondage of some of those who escaped slavery via the Underground Railroad. Mr. Still was an African American who was charged by the Pennsylvania Anti-Slavery Society to "compile and publish his personal reminiscences and experiences relating to the Underground Rail Road." He took his work seriously. His compelling narratives of slave arrivals are often accompanied by the newspaper advertisements requesting the return of the runaways in question.

The author took great pains to describe the physical appearance of those seeking freedom. For example:

Chaskey is about twenty-four years of age, quite black, medium size, sound body and intelligent appearance, nevertheless he resembled a "farm hand" in every particular.

Perry was about thirty-one years of age, round-made, of dark complexion.

Susan, who was in Mary's charge, was an invalid child of four years of age, who never walked and whose mother had escaped to Canada abut three years before under circumstances which obliged her to leave this child, then only a year old.

Emanuel was about twenty-five years of age, with seven-eighths of white blood in his veins, medium size and a very smart and likely-looking piece of property.

Anthony was thirty-six years of age, and by blood, was quite as nearly related to the Anglo-Saxon as to the Anglo-African. He was nevertheless, physically a fine specimen of a man. He was about six feet high.

If you find any ancestors' names recorded in Still's book, you will learn a great deal about them, including the name of the person who owned them, how and when they escaped, where they escaped to, and, in most cases, the plantations they lived on when enslaved. With this information, you may well be able to find your way back to your earliest African-American ancestors. Even if you do not find their names in his work, however, *The Underground Rail Road* is well worth reading. The firsthand accounts of slavery and the pursuit of freedom underscore the courage and determination that are part of our African-American legacy.

HERE SHE IS! WHERE?

You've done it all. You started with your present and worked your way back as far as you could. Along the way you may well have discovered more about your family than you realized there was to know. And your hard work has paid off. You found that African who is at the foundation of your family in this country. Perhaps the key for you was an old name that has been in your family for generations—a name that identified this African forebear. Perhaps you were lucky enough to ferret out the name of a slave owner who purchased your ancestor, or found in some historical society the plantation records that told you when and where your forebear was purchased. Maybe several members of your family remembered the name of the ship that carried your ancestor to this country and knew where it docked. Someone may have handed over a manumission paper or told you how your African-American ancestor escaped using the Underground Railroad. However you found your earliest African-American forebear, know how lucky you are! The number of us who can actually trace our roots back to Africa could probably fit quite comfortably in a few slave shacks on some plantation.

On the other hand, you may be one of those who, despite all your hard work, has not come up with that man, woman, boy, or girl—that African—who is the foundation of your family in this country. Right now all you want to know is where *your* people are. Think of how wonderful that expectation is with its implicit demand: I want to find my African forebears, now! Less than a lifetime ago, James Brown was demanding that we "say it loud! I'm Black and I'm proud!" Less than a lifetime ago, we couldn't find ourselves portrayed in a single elementary school textbook; less than a lifetime ago, almost nobody talked about finding African forebears.

I have been looking for my African-American forebears for longer than I want to think about. Sometimes I have to give the search a rest. At other times I give my worksheets or charts a once-over lightly and see something new. For example, my great-great-grandparents acquired property in Whippany, New Jersey, in 1868. I've known this forever. I also knew that they had been living on that property for some time before it became theirs in 1868. 1868. 1868. One day, out of the clear blue, I realized that I had read somewhere about a historical map showing Whippany, New Jersey, in 1868. A copy of this map is now proudly displayed in our home. Like many maps of the period, the names of homeowners are shown to indicate where they lived. The 1868 Whippany map carries my great-great-grandfather's name and shows the spot where he and his family made their home. Charles Thompson is not the African I am looking for. Nor is Ellen Thompson, the woman I believe to be his mother, who was born in 1804. Still, this map is one more document that supports a Thompson presence in this town—a document more than 125 years old.

At times you may need to take a break from your own research. At other times you will need to study your notes for clues you may have missed the first, second, third, or even fourth time around. You may need to revisit relatives or places to add to or clarify the information you have. And you may need to remind yourself that you are in it for the long haul. Then you can relax and permit yourself to revel in every discovery you make about your family while you are looking for your earliest African-American ancestors.

In truth, I want to find my African forebears, too! As long as I have sight and sanity, I will continue to look for them. At some point I may have to admit to myself that the records I need to find them, to prove they belong to me and I to them, were never kept or no longer exist. At some point I may have to tell myself that no griot is waiting in some African village to tell me how a forebear disappeared one warm summer day and was never seen again. Still, as a student of history, I know scholars are uncovering new research every day. More often than we notice, someone finds information that sheds new light on old mysteries. Perhaps some slave ship captain's descendant is holding on to diaries detailing each of his voyages to and from Africa—diaries that listed his human cargo by both their African names and the names they were given when sold in this country. Perhaps stacks of plantation records are collecting dust in some attic—records that detail the buying and selling of slaves who happen to include your forebears or mine. Or, more likely, a relative will suddenly remember something he was told that provides *the* missing connection between now and then. All these possibilities and countless others exist. Be open to them.

10

Keeping Your Family's Story Alive

 There will come a point in your search for your roots when you realize that you have accumulated a great deal of valuable information about your family—information that may have been, before you came along, simply bits and pieces of various things scattered in many kinds of places, in many parts of the country. Even if you have found the Africans who established your family in this country, you may feel you have just scratched the surface of all there is to learn about your forebears. Still, you are anxious to share some of your discoveries with other members of your family. You may wonder just how much more you have to do before you can feel comfortable in telling others at least part of your family's story. The truth is that no matter where you are in your search for your roots, there is no reason to delay sharing what you have learned.

OFFERING GLIMPSES INTO THE PAST

Family members who have not shared in your search for your African-American ancestors may have no idea of the kinds of information you have uncovered. Some may think you have spent most of your time in libraries or courthouses, hunching over boring old documents, all to no purpose. In truth, there may have been moments when you felt this way, too! Still, imagine their surprise when you share some of the exciting images or artifacts that help document your common past.

One way to begin sharing your discoveries with family members might be to select one or two of the most intriguing images you have found, have them copied, and distribute them among family members. For example, you might choose to share a photograph of a grandmother on her wedding day. This will be especially treasured by those who have known her only as an older person. Or you may wish to have copies made of a manumission paper that belonged to a forebear who bought his freedom before the Civil War. These copies can be framed and distributed to family members along with a brief description of this particular ancestor and some of his accomplishments. Or perhaps you have found a letter written by a great-grandmother that tells something of her work as a small-business owner in the early twentieth century. Framed copies of a page or two of such a letter would make a wonderful holiday or special-occasion gift for family members who share your interest in historical documents.

In your search for your roots, you may have videotaped a family home place that everyone talks about but few have seen. You could arrange a special showing of this video at a family gathering, or have the tape reproduced for those who might be interested. You may even select an especially attractive frame from the video to produce as a single photograph that could be copied and shared.

As you can see, the opportunities to offer family members glimpses into your common past are limited only by your imagination and creativity. Do not be surprised if these glimpses lead to requests for more information. The excitement that comes with searching for roots is often contagious.

PREPARING A WRITTEN FAMILY HISTORY

Of all the choices open to you in sharing your family's story, framing a few photos or documents is probably easiest. If you decide to record everything you have discovered so far, however, it may make the most sense to prepare a family history. No matter how incomplete this history is, the work you have done is valuable and should be written down. Moreover, you will find that, once completed, your written family history can serve a number of purposes. Once reproduced, it can be mailed to relatives or handed out at family gatherings; it can also be shared with people outside your family, including local historical groups, schools, libraries, archives, and other area research centers. Using your computer and an online service, you can share your family history on the Internet, inviting any relatives who are "out there" to come online with research they may have done that relates to the family you have in common.

Once in printed form, you can use your family history as the basis for an attractive video package. Although producing a satisfactory video will take time and be somewhat expensive, you should have no trouble finding a local video house to help you meet production challenges. You can even enroll in a video course at your local community college and complete a family history video as part of your course work, using your written history as an outline or script for the video you produce.

My decision to prepare a family history was triggered by a very small thing. My brother picked up a photograph of our grandfather, which I keep on a table along with dozens of other family photos, and said, "Daddy dressed nicely, didn't he?"

"That's not Daddy," I answered. "That's Poppy." Granted, our father and grandfather looked a great deal alike, but they were not identical. Since my brother was a teen when our grandfather died, he had known Poppy well. Still, almost twenty years had passed since our grandfather's death, and in that time my brother had lost his ability to identify him in a photograph. At that moment I decided to prepare a special Christmas gift for my siblings and our children—a family history that would include photographs I had collected from relatives and friends; wills, deeds, maps, and other documents that shed some light on our family's story; birth, marriage, and death certificates that gave a human dimension to our family. Realizing that too many family histories omit items that would be of significance to descendants, I decided also to include a few pages showing people and places that were important to my siblings and me in our own lifetimes.

Having spent my professional life in publishing prepared me to write a family history. I completed most of the work using my old and comfortable personal computer, which is equipped with an adequate word-processing program. I did not own a scanner that would copy and position graphics; for a modest fee, however, a local graphics house did this job for me, as well as designing an inexpensive but attractive cover and binding the twenty-five copies I requested. The total cost for the work was less than five hundred dollars and less than I would have spent for the Christmas gifts the booklet replaced. My siblings were overjoyed with the gift. Our children were awestruck. One said, "I knew we'd always been in Whippany but I didn't know we'd *always* been in Whippany."

What if you don't own a computer with word-processing capability or even a typewriter? What if you don't know how to type? Don't despair. There are countless individuals and one- or two-person enterprises that specialize in processing handwritten documents, turning them into attractive, typeset pages. If you decide to have someone assist you in this way, be prepared to explain how you would like the finished product to look. If you are not sure of the possibilities, do not hesitate to ask for suggestions. The person you choose to help you should be prepared to show you samples of what can be done. If you run across copies of other family histories that you find attractive, show them to the person who will be helping you. You may find it too expensive or time consuming to incorporate all the ideas you glean from other family histories into your own, but you can certainly borrow some that appeal to you.

Reversing the Process

When you began tracing your roots, you started with the present and worked your way back toward your earliest African-American ancestors. When you are preparing a family history, you will want to reverse this process: Your story should begin with the earliest ancestors you found. Again, do not despair if you can go back only as far as one great-grandparent. If you have been able to do this, you have traced four generations of one branch of your family. If you have children of your own, having found one great-grandparent enables you to account for five generations. That is quite an accomplishment. A hundred years from now, using the work you have done, your descendants may well be able to trace their roots back eight or nine generations. Even more exciting, one of these descendants, building on your work, may find your family's earliest African-American ancestor, if you have not already done so, or identify other ancestors who also represent early and important branches of your family.

To help you know how to put your family's story into a good form, you may want to consult one of the books that writers and editors use to guide their work. Either *Words Into Type,* published by Prentice Hall, Inc., or *The Chicago Manual of Style,* published by the University of Chicago Press, will help you find your way through any number of writing challenges. Many writers would not be without William Strunk Jr. and E. B. White's *Elements of Style,* published by Macmillan Publishing Co., Inc. This slim volume includes much of what you need know to help you make your writing lucid and engaging.

Beginning With History

It would be wise to begin your family's story with some history of the times in which the ancestors you found were living. The history you provide will come naturally from the research you have done and need not fill more than a page or two. For example, it has been estimated that in a single year, 1879, forty thousand African Americans who lived in the South fled to the Midwest to escape the harsh political and economic realities of Reconstruction. If your family was among them, those who read your history may find it interesting to know something about the Reconstruction period that followed the Civil War. Some of your forebears may have been among those pioneer families that helped settle the West. Their hardships and their triumphs should be shared as part of your family's story. Perhaps a great-grandfather was a famed Tuskegee airman or the first member of your family to earn a college degree. Those who read your family's history should know something of the challenges these forebears met and overcame.

While some African Americans found that their lives little changed after slavery, for others freedom meant attending school for the first time, starting their own businesses, or acquiring property in their own names. Whatever your ancestors' accomplishments, however, all African Americans were affected in some ways by the segregated society they lived in. The family history you write should help your readers understand the significance of segregation and the ways it affected your family.

A textbook of U.S. history will help you present your family in the context of its times. Some history texts, however, are not complete enough to include events important to African Americans. To get a more balanced picture, you may want to consult a text that deals with African-American history or chronology. *Books in Print,* published by R. R. Bowker, includes listings of the African-American history texts currently available. Among those you might consider is *Chronology of African-American History: Significant Events and People From 1619 to the Present* by Alton Hornsby Jr. (see bibliography). This book is readable, simply organized, and includes a fairly lengthy introduction that summarizes at least in part the African-American experience in the United States. Remember, you are consulting an African-American history text to bring balance to your family's story. Any work that has an African-American bias is as problematic for the genealogist as one that excludes African Americans. It will be important for the relatives who read your family history—those living today and those who will be around in the next century—to be as informed about the American part of their heritage as they are about the African part.

Finally, it should not be your intent to overwhelm your readers with history, either African or American, but rather to help them understand a little of the influences that surrounded your family in this country. You can be sure that if a particular period or incident interests them, they will investigate on their own.

Organizing by Generation

As I have mentioned, your family history will be understood most easily if your organize the material by generation, starting with the earliest you have been able to uncover. If you can trace your family back four generations, your family history will have at least four sections, one for each generation. If you can trace your family back seven generations, you will have at least seven sections in your family history. For each generation, include some of what you have discovered about their work, their religious activities, their social involvements, the houses and towns and states they lived in, any illnesses they may have endured, and their deaths, including the places of burial. Include a genealogical chart for each generation. If you are writing about your great-great-grandparents, the genealogical chart in their section of the family history will show them at the top and you or your children at the bottom. (You may want to review the information in chapter 2 and the genealogical charts you have included among your Individual Family Worksheets.) Remember to designate each chart by surname, which will identify a particular branch of your family.

You may have discovered several branches of your family in a given generation. If this is the case, you will want to say something about how these branches are related; be sure that the genealogical charts that pertain to them highlight these relationships.

Including Anecdotal Material

One of the things that will make your family history unique is the anecdotal material you include. Was one of your forebears a barber who was privy to all the secrets in town? Did a widowed grandfather leave all his worldly goods to a woman no one had ever heard of before his will was read? Did a maiden aunt run off with a man who came to town with a medicine show? Your notes from family interviews will doubtless include anecdotes you will want to share. If not, ask your relatives to supply a few. For instance, my father used to call me Jeff, because the correct answer to a telephone quiz (one that would have entitled us to the handsome sum of twenty-five dollars) was John Adams—and I responded, "Thomas Jefferson." "How are you doing today, Jeff? Have you had enough to eat, Jeff? You look nice today, Jeff." The anecdotal materials you include in your family history are sure to bring pleasure to your readers for generations to come, and some feeling for the people who are members of their family.

Using Graphics

Today's reproduction facilities will enable you to get copies of virtually anything—photographs, wills, deeds, certificates, newspaper clippings, diplomas, historical maps, and funeral programs. Include as many of these items in your family history as you can. Each document will help show your family in a particular time, place, and circumstance. Photographs can be especially informative. Styles of dress, household furnishings, and common items shown in yards, such as washtubs and curtain stretchers, can convey important information about the ordinary incidents in your ancestors' lives. When you choose a company to reproduce your valuable photographs or documents, be sure it has experience in working with old materials and understands the importance of safeguarding your treasures.

Make sure captions are clear and provide the information your readers need to understand who or what is being shown. For example, under a photograph of your grandmother, you might write: MARY WILSON SMITH (1919–1996). Somewhere in your history you will have discussed her, so that when your readers see her photograph they will be able to connect an image with a particular set of facts. Remember, always include the maiden name for all your female forebears. When writing a caption, if you are not sure about a maiden name but have a good idea of what it was, simply write MARY (WILSON?) SMITH.

Knowing When It Is "Right"

Writing is not an easy task. You may worry about getting your family history "right." In the final analysis, though, there is no "right" or "wrong" way to do a family history. Some things are, of course, more important than others. As much as you can, be sure the facts you share about your family are correct. When you are not sure of something, do not be afraid to say so. Your candor may encourage someone else to pick up the ball and help you find the answers you need. You may feel uncomfortable writing about incidents you find embarrassing. Perhaps you do not want to mention that one forebear was born to an unwed mother, another was lynched, or still another was an alcoholic.

If discussing those things makes you feel uncomfortable, do not discuss them. This is your version of your family history. You are completely free to include or exclude anything you choose. However, out of respect for the hard work you have done and in fairness to the members of your family who will benefit from this difficult labor, make sure any information you do choose to include is as truthful as possible. To do otherwise does you and your family a disservice.

When all is said and done, our family histories are not about embarrassing incidents, despite the fact that every family has its fair share of them. These histories are about how our ancestors met the challenges life dealt them. You can be assured that your descendants' lives are not likely to be enriched by discovering that an ancestor was born on the wrong side of the blanket. These descendants may find enrichment, however, in learning that an ancestor or two survived by making blankets or shoeing horses or teaching children or escaping to freedom. Sharing these accomplishments and others like them will make your family's history "right."

Buying an Existing History
Once you decide to write your family's history, you may find yourself prey to any number of individuals or groups who assure you that this work has already been done. At least once or twice each year I receive letters offering me the opportunity to buy a history of my family covering a period of more than a hundred years. The offer letter, always touting a "never-before-published book," tells me that those sharing my family name were recorded in the first census, migrated across America, and described their journeys in

letters and diaries, all of which are recorded in the book being offered.

The latest such letter I received assured me that "this outstanding collection of current and historical information" is available nowhere else. To make sure I would be left salivating, I was told that I am listed in this heirloom-quality, handmade, and elaborately illustrated book. Then, finally, "This is the only publication of its kind in the entire world and you will want to have your own copy to share with your loved ones. Please note, however, that you must order now."

If you yield to temptation and order a book of this kind, you will still have two choices: You can take advantage of the "simply return it" offer when you find the book has nothing to do with your family; or you can put the book on a shelf, knowing you have helped some budding entrepreneur meet his or her quarterly sales goals. Whichever option you choose, *your* family history will still have to be written. Why not start on it while you're waiting for that "heirloom-quality" book to arrive at your front door?

RELIVING YOUR HISTORY

One of the best ways to keep your family's history alive is by relating it at every opportunity and to a variety of audiences. Because you have done so much research, you are especially well equipped for the task. You may be the only one in your family who knows that a forebear was helped to freedom by a member of the slave owner's family, or that there is no history of slavery in several branches of your family. Spread the word. The more people you tell about your discoveries, the better chance you have of finding someone who can add to them.

Family Gatherings
Family gatherings and reunions are ideal settings for sharing old stories that pertain to your family, and for learning new ones. Family gatherings are also good places to find answers to some of the ques-

tions you have about your family. If you have found a name you cannot pin down or a photograph of people you do not recognize, take this with you when you meet with family members.

When looking though family papers, I once found a very old photograph, obviously posed, of four children in a yard. One was sitting in a charming high chair and the others were standing around her. I passed the picture around at a Thanksgiving dinner. One of the aunts in attendance exclaimed: "I've been wondering what happened to this picture!"

"Do you know who they are?" I asked.

"Of course I do! It's Pop, Aunt Stacia, Aunt Liz, and Aunt Marge. This was taken on Aunt Liz's first birthday."

Once they were identified, I knew the rest of the story. The children in the photograph were siblings. The Aunt Liz in question was my great-aunt Elizabeth, born in 1895. Pop was my grandfather, born in 1891; Aunt Stacia was born in 1877, Aunt Marge in 1884.

I have pinned down other photos in exactly the same way. In all likelihood, you will be able to do the same. Indeed, you may want to have copies of old photographs made for just this purpose. I have found that even though most folks will try to clean their hands before picking up a photograph or document, barbecue sauce has a way of clinging to fingers and attaching itself to whatever it touches. Therefore, you will always want to pass around copies, never cherished originals.

Encourage storytelling at family gatherings and, although you have now become something of a griot, be sure to listen to others. You may hear something you have never heard before, and this something may well be another part of the puzzle that is your family. Be sure to include the youngest members of your family in storytelling. They are your family's future, and the things they hear about their family are likely to be repeated to their children and grandchildren. Share information in a way they are likely to remember. For example, "Your great-great-great-grandfather—that's three *greats,* kid—was the first African American to own his own business right here in town. He repaired wagons and buggies." A young person hearing this story will be sure to remember the phrase *that's three* greats, *kid!* And this will help him remember the rest of the tale.

Public Appearances

You can keep your family's history alive by sharing it with others at special school assemblies, at meetings of your local historical society, and at certain church-sponsored functions. Service organizations and library groups are always looking for speakers. Black History Month, celebrated in February of each year, is an ideal time to begin this activity. Once you are known, expect to be asked to share your family's history at other times during the year.

Most organizations begin their program year in September. This would be a good time to write to a school principal or society president about your availability to present a unique program on African Americans during Black History Month. Tell her a little about what you would like to discuss and indicate your willingness meet with the program director. If the school class or civic group you want to address is located in your hometown, you are likely to be given a chance to speak—probably for a half hour or less. Still, you can say a great deal about your family in a half hour.

Moreover, once you have spoken in one place, you are likely to find yourself in demand in others. There are still countless people who want to know how to go about tracing their roots. You can serve as a valuable resource for them. Your remarks will be enhanced if you have slides of old photographs or documents and are able to share your excitement with others. If you have prepared a family history, you may wish to leave a copy behind for use in a library or research room.

Many local cable television stations grant the public access to airwaves. You should be able to schedule a time to tell your family's story via this station. You may want to enlist the aid of family members in putting together a program that will be appealing to a television audience. Members of your family may also want to participate in this on-camera experience. Program managers at local radio stations may also be interested in granting you time to tell something of your family's story, especially if that story is perceived as interesting. You may be allotted only a few minutes but you can do a lot in that period of time, especially if you make use of amusing or interesting anecdotal material.

Take advantage of every opportunity you have to share your joy in knowing something of your African-American roots. If you are enthusiastic in presenting your materials, other people will feel and appreciate your joy. In fact, this joy may be contagious enough to get others started on their own searches for African-American ancestors.

TAKING OUR PAST INTO OUR FUTURE

When our earliest African-American forebears looked toward their future, they must have dreamed of a good, perhaps a better, life for themselves and their descendants. As the twenty-first century dawns, many African Americans dream, as did their ancestors, of a better life. In some areas of the United States racism is as prevalent and as virulent as it has ever been. But we are stronger today than we have ever been. A great deal of this strength comes from knowing who we are. No matter how far back you have been able to trace your roots, you have found forebears who faced enormous challenges and persevered. Whatever their accomplishments, our African-American ancestors have passed on to us a history of survival and success that can be celebrated, emulated, and shared.

You are not the same person you were when you began to trace your African-American roots. You are prouder of who you are and where you came from. Your past is now part of you, and it will inform and influence your future in unexpected ways. You will find it difficult to stop looking for your ancestors because you know each one you find will have something positive to share. And you will want to talk with others about your forebears because so much about them is relevant to the lives we live today. The experiences and triumphs of African Americans in the United States have been breathtaking, and you and your family are part of them.

Whatever your background or accomplishments, having traced your roots means you will never again look at other African Americans as you perceived them before. You now know each of us has a story to tell and perhaps some of our stories are the same. Your forebears and mine may have come from the same African village. My ancestors and yours may have shared hardships and hopes while living on the same plantation. One thing is clear: We each carry our past into our future. Only we can decide if this past will cause us to reach out to and support each other in our continuing search for those African Americans who established our families in this country.

Appendix I

State Offices of Vital Records

The following listing includes the location of state offices of vital records and fees charged (at this writing) for copies of birth, death, marriage, and divorce records. For example, the state of Alaska currently charges ten dollars for a copy of a marriage record. Arkansas currently charges four dollars for a copy of a death record. Fees change. Be sure to confirm the fee for the specific documents you wish to receive.

The dates shown in parentheses are those for which specific records are available. For example, the state of Alabama has birth records dating from 1908; Iowa has death records dating from 1800.

If an event—a marriage, for example—is followed by the words *county records,* you must look for those records in the county in which the event took place.

Alabama
Alabama Center for Health
  Statistics
Office of Vital Records
Montgomery, AL 36111
(334) 206-5418
Birth: $12.00 (from 1908)
Death: $12.00 (from 1908)
Marriage: $12.00 (from 1936)
Divorce: $12.00 (from 1950)

Alaska
Alaska Department of Health
  and Social Services
P.O. Box 110675
Juneau, AK 99811-0675
(907) 465-3038
Fax: (907) 465-3618
Birth: $10.00 (from 1913)
Death: $10.00 (from 1913)
Marriage: $10.00 (from 1913)
Divorce: $10.00 (from 1913)

Arizona
Arizona State Office of Vital
  Records
P.O. Box 3887
Phoenix, AZ 85030
(602) 255-2501
Fax: (602) 249-3040
Birth: $9.00 (before 1950);
  $6.00 (after 1950)
Death: $6.00 (from 1887)
Marriage: County records
Divorce: County records

Arkansas
Arkansas Vital Records
4815 West Markham Street
Little Rock, AR 72205
(501) 661-2637
Birth: $5.00 (from 1914)
Death: $4.00 (from 1917)
Marriage: $5.00 (from 1917)
Divorce: $5.00 (from 1923)

California
California Office of the State
  Registrar of Vital Statistics
304 "S" Street
Sacramento, CA 95814-0241
(916) 445-2684
Fax: 1-800-858-5553 (with credit
  card charge)
Birth: $12.00 (from 1905)
Death: $8.00 (from 1905)
Marriage: $12.00 from 1905
  through 1986; from 1987,
  county records
Divorce: County records

Colorado
Colorado Department of Public
  Health and Environment

Vital Records Section
4300 Cherry Creek Drive South
Denver, CO 80222-1530
(303) 756-4464
Fax: 1-800-423-1108
Birth: $15.00 (from 1900)
Death: $15.00 (from 1900)
Marriage: County records
  (verification only; 1900 through
  1939 and from 1975)
Divorce: County records

Connecticut
Connecticut Department of Public
  Health and Addiction Services
Vital Records Unit
150 Washington Street
Hartford, CT 06106
(203) 509-7899
(The Connecticut State
  Department no longer provides
  a central records service.
  Contact the town in which the
  birth, death, marriage, or
  divorce occurred. Dates of
  record availability vary from
  town to town. A flat fee of $5.00
  is charged for each inquiry.
  Contact the Department of
  Public Health only if you need
  additional information about the
  person to contact for the town
  in which the event occurred.)

Delaware
Delaware Office of Vital Statistics
P.O. Box 637
Dover, DE 19903
(302) 739-4721
Birth: $6.00 (from 1924)
Death: $6.00 (from 1956)

Marriage: $6:00 (from 1956)
Divorce: N/A

District of Columbia
District of Columbia Vital Records
   Branch
800 Ninth Street SW, First Floor
Washington, DC 20024
(202) 645-5909
Birth: $12.00 (from 1894)
Death: $12.00 computer copies;
   $18.00 copies of original (from
   1874)
Marriage: City records
Divorce: City records: D.C.
   Superior Court
500 Indiana Avenue, NW

Florida
Florida Department of HRS
Office of Vital Statistics
P.O. Box 210
Jacksonville, FL 32231-0042
(904) 359-6900
Fax: (904) 359-6993
Birth: $10.00 (from 1865)
Death: $5.00 (from 1877)
Marriage: $5.00 (from 1927)
Divorce: $5.00 (from 1927)

Georgia
Georgia Division of Public Health:
   Vital Records Service
Room 217-H
47 Trinity Avenue SW
Atlanta, GA 30334-5600
(404) 656-4750
Birth: $10.00 (from 1919)
Death: $10.00 (from 1919)
Marriage: $10.00 (from 1952)
Divorce: County records

Hawaii
Hawaii State Department
   of Health
Vital Records
P.O. Box 3378
Honolulu, HI 96801
(808) 586-4539
Birth: $10.00 (from 1910)
Death: $10.00 (from 1910)
Marriage: $10.00 (from 1910)
Divorce: $10.00 (from 1910)
(Written requests only; no phone
   verifications.)

Idaho
Idaho Center for Vital Statistics
   and Health Policy
450 West State Street, First Floor
Boise, ID 83720-0036
(208) 334-5976
Fax: (208) 389-9096 (with credit
   card charge)
Birth: $10.00 (from 1911)
Death: $10.00 (from 1911)
Marriage: $10.00 (from 1947)
Divorce: $10.00 (from 1947)

Illinois
Illinois Department of Public
   Health
Division of Vital Records
605 West Jefferson
Springfield, IL 62702-5097
(217) 782-6554
Fax: (217) 523-2648 (with credit
   card charge)
Birth: $15.00 (from 1916)
Death: $10.00; certified copy
   $15.00 (from 1916)
Marriage and Divorce: $5.00
   (verification only; from 1962)

Indiana
Indiana State Department
  of Health
P.O. Box 7125
Indianapolis, IN 46206-7125
(317) 233-1325
(317) 233-2700 (with credit card
  charge)
Fax: (317) 383-62 10 (with credit
  card charge)
Birth: $6.00 (from 1907)
Death: $4.00 (from 1907)
Marriage: County records
Divorce: County records

Iowa
Iowa Department of Public Health:
  Vital Statistics
321 East Twelfth
Des Moines, IA 50319
(515) 255-2414
Birth: $10.00 (from 1880)
Death: $10.00 (from 1800)
Marriage: $10.00 (from 1880)
Divorce: County records

Kansas
Kansas Office of Vital Statistics
900 SW Jackson
Topeka, KS 66612-2221
(913) 296-1400
Fax: (913) 357-4332 (with credit
  card charge)
Birth: $10.00 (from 1913)
Death: $10.00 (from 1911)
Marriage: $10.00 (from 1913)
Divorce: $10.00 (from 1951)

Kentucky
Kentucky Vital Statistics
275 East Main Street

Frankfort, KY 40621
Birth: $9.00 (from 1911)
Death: $6.00 (from 1911)
Marriage: $6.00 (from 1958)
Divorce: $6.00 (from 1958)

Louisiana
Louisiana Vital Records Registry
P.O. Box 60630
New Orleans, LA 70160
(504) 568-5150
(504) 568-5152
Fax: (504) 568-5391 (with credit
  card charge)
Birth: $15.00 (from 1898)
Death: $5.00 (from 1948)
Marriage: Parish records: $5.00
  (from 1948)
Divorce: N/A (except Orleans
  Parish)

Maine
Maine Vital Records
221 State Street, Station 11
Augusta, ME 04333-0011
(207) 287-3181
Fax: (207) 287-1097 (with credit
  card charge)
Birth: $10.00 (from 1923)
Death: $10.00 (from 1923)
Marriage: $10.00 (from 1923)
Divorce: $10.00 (from 1923)

Maryland
Maryland Division of Vital
  Records
4201 Patterson Avenue
Baltimore, MD 21215
(410) 764-3028
Fax: (410) 358-0781 (with credit
  card charge)

Birth: $4.00 (from 1875)
Death: $4.00 (from 1969)
Marriage: $4.00 (from 1951)
Divorce: Verification only
   (from 1962)

Michigan
Michigan Department of
   Community Health
3423 Martin Luther King Blvd
P.O. Box 30195
Lansing, MI 48909
(517) 335-8656
Fax: (517) 335-8666
Birth: $13.00 (from 1867)
Death: $13.00 (from 1867)
Marriage: $13.00 (from 1897)
Divorce: $13.00 (from 1867)

Minnesota
Minnesota Department of
   Health
717 Delaware Street SE
Minneapolis, MN 55414
(612) 623-5121
Fax: (612) 331-5776 (with credit
   card charge)
Birth: $14.00 (from 1900)
Death: $11.00 (from 1908)
Marriage: County records
Divorce: County records

Mississippi
Mississippi Vital Records
P.O. Box 1700
Jackson, MS 39215
(601) 960-7981
Fax: (601) 354-6174 (with credit
   card charge)
Birth: $12.00 (from 1912)
Death: $10.00 (from 1912)

Marriage:$10.00 (from 1926; no
   records for July 1938 through
   December 31, 1941)
Divorce: County records

Missouri
Missouri Department of Health
Bureau of Vital Records
P.O. Box 570
Jefferson City, MO 65102
(573) 751-6387
Birth: $10.00 (from 1910; earlier
   certificates available for an
   additional $10.00 search
   charge)
Death: $10.00 (from 1910)
Marriage: Free (from July 1948)
Divorce: Free (from July 1948)

Montana
Montana Department of Public
   Health and Human Services
111 North Sanders #215
Helena, MT 59620
(406) 444-4228
Birth: $10.00 (from 1907)
Death: $10.00 (from 1907)
Marriage: County records
   (from 1943)
Divorce: County records
   (from 1943)

Nebraska
Nebraska State Department of
   Health
Health Records Management Vital
   Records Unit
P.O. Box 95065
Lincoln, NE 68509-5065
(402) 471-2871
Birth: $10.00 (from 1904)

Death: $9.00 (from 1904)
Marriage: $9.00 (from 1909)
Divorce: $9.00 (from 1909)
(Credit card charges may be made
    through an automated recorded
    message system.)

Nevada
Nevada Office of Vital Statistics
505 East King Street
Carson City, NV 89710
(702) 687-4480
Birth: $11.00 (from 1911)
Death: $8.00 (from 1911)
Marriage: County records
Divorce: County records

New Hampshire
New Hampshire Bureau of Vital
    Records and Health Statistics
Division of Public Health
Health and Welfare Building
6 Hazen Drive
Concord, NH 03301-6527
(603) 271-4650 (credit card may
    be used with service fee)
Birth: $10.00 (from 1640)
Death: $10.00 (from 1640)
Marriage: $10.00 (from 1640)
Divorce: $10.00 (from 1640)

New Jersey
New Jersey Bureau of Vital
    Statistics
CN 370 Room 504
Trenton, NJ 08625
(609) 292-4087
(609) 633-2860 (Vital Check:
    $5.00) [This permits you to
    telephone in your request for a

record of birth, death, or
    marriage information]
Fax: (609) 392-4292
Birth: $4.00 (from 1878)
Death: $4.00 (from 1878)
Marriage: $4.00 (from 1878)
Divorce: N/A

New Mexico
New Mexico Bureau of Vital
    Records and Health
    Statistics
1190 St. Francis Drive
P.O. Box 26110
Santa Fe, NM 87502
(505) 827-0121
(505) 827-2316 (with credit card
    charge)
Fax: (505) 984-1048
Birth: $10.00 (from 1919; a few
    available prior to 1919)
Death: $5.00 (from 1919; a few
    available prior to 1919)
Marriage: County records
Divorce: County records

New York
New York State Department
    of Health
Empire State Plaza
Albany, NY 12237-0023
(518) 474-3055
Fax: (518) 474-3077 (Automated
    system for birth certificates
    only.)
Birth: $15.00 (from 1880)
Death: $15.00 (from 1880)
Marriage: $5.00 (from 1880)
Divorce: $15.00 (from 1880)
(Payment by money order only.)

New York City
Bureau of Vital Records
125 Worth Street
New York, NY 10013
(212) 669-8898
(Costs are the same as those in
  New York State, except marriage
  records, which are $15.00.)

North Carolina
North Carolina Vital Records
P.O. Box 29537
Raleigh, NC 27626
(919) 733-3000
Birth: $10.00 (from 1913)
Death: $10.00 (from 1930)
Marriage: $10.00 (from 1962)
Divorce: $10.00 (from 1958)

North Dakota
North Dakota Vital Records
State Capitol
600 East Boulevard Avenue
Bismarck, ND 58505-0200
(701) 328-2360
Birth: $7.00 (from 1870)
Death: $5.00 (from 1881)
Marriage: $5.00 (from July 1925;
  for earlier dates check with
  county)
Divorce: County records

Ohio
Ohio Department of Health
Vital Statistics
P.O. Box 15098
Columbus, OH 43215-0098
(614) 466-2531
Birth: $7.00 (from 1908)
Death: $7.00 (from 1945)

Marriage: County records
Divorce: County records

Oklahoma
Oklahoma State Health Department
Division of Vital Records
1000 NE Tenth Street
Oklahoma City, OK 73152
(405) 271-4040
Birth: $5.00 (from 1908)
Death: $10.00 (from 1908)
Marriage: County records
Divorce: County records

Oregon
Oregon Health Division
Vital Records
P.O. Box 14050
Portland, OR 97293
(503) 731-4108
(503) 234-8417 (with credit card
  charge)
Birth: $15.00 (from 1903)
Death: $15.00 (from 1903)
Marriage: $15.00 (from 1906)
Divorce: $15.00 (from 1925)
(By mail use money order only.)

Pennsylvania
Pennsylvania Division of Vital
  Records
P.O. Box 1528
New Castle, PA 16103
(412) 656-3100
Fax: (412) 652-8951 (with credit
  card charge)
Birth: $4.00 (from 1906)
Death: $3.00 (from 1906)
Marriage: County records
Divorce: County records

Rhode Island
Rhode Island Department
of Health
3 Capitol Hill, Room 101
Providence, RI 02908-5097
(401) 277-2812
Birth: $15.00 (from 1894)
Death: $15.00 (from 1944)
Marriage: $15.00 (from 1894)
Divorce: County records

South Carolina
South Carolina Vital Records
2600 Bull Street
Columbia, SC 29201
(803) 734-4810
(803) 734-6663 (with credit card
charge)
Birth: $8.00 (from 1915)
Death: $15.00 (from 1915)
Marriage: $15.00 (from 1950)
Divorce: $8.00 (from 1962)

South Dakota
South Dakota Department
of Health
c/o Vital Statistics
600 East Capitol Avenue
Pierre, SD 57501-3185
(605) 773-4961
Birth: $7.00 (from 1905; some
prior)
Death: $7.00 (from 1905)
Marriage: $7.00 (from 1905)
Divorce: $7.00 (from 1905

Tennessee
Tennessee Vital Records
Third Floor
Tennessee Towers Building
Nashville, TN 37247-0350

(615) 741-1763
(615) 741-0778 (with credit card
charge)
Fax: (615) 726-2559
Birth: $10.00 (from 1914; some
prior)
Death: $5.00 (from July 1944)
Marriage: $10.00 (from July 1944)
Divorce: $10.00 (from July 1944)

Texas
Texas Department of Health
Vital Records
P.O. Box 12040
Austin, TX 78711-2040
(512) 458-7111, ext. 3184
Fax: (512) 458-7711 (with credit
card charge)
Birth: $11.00 (from 1903)
Death: $9.00 (from 1903)
Marriage: County records
Divorce: County records

Utah
Utah Bureau of Records
288 North 1460 West
Box 142855
Salt Lake City, UT 84114-2855
(801) 538-6380
(Use the same number with a
credit card for a $15.00 service
charge.)
Birth: $12.00 (from 1905)
Death: $9.00 (from 1905)
Marriage: County records
Divorce: County records

Vermont
From 1988
Vermont Department of Health:
Vital Records

P.O. Box 70
Burlington, VT 05402
(802) 863-7275
Birth: $7.00
Death: $7.00
Marriage: $7.00
Divorce: $7.00
Prior to 1988
General Services Center
Public Records Division
U.S. Route 2, Middlesex
Drawer 22
Montpelier, VT 05633-7601
(802) 828-3286
Fax: (802) 828-3710 (for
    genealogy information only;
    service charge)
Birth: $7.00 (from 1760)
Death: $7.00 (from 1760)
Marriage: $7.00 (from 1760)
Divorce: $7.00 (from 1760)

Virginia
Virginia Division of Vital
    Records
P.O. Box 1000
Richmond, VA 23218-1000
(804) 644-2537 (Vital Check, with
    credit card charge. Vital Check
    permits you to telephone in
    your request for a record of
    birth, death, or marriage
    information.)
Fax: (804) 644-2550
Birth: $8.00 (from 1853)
Death: $8.00 (from 1853)
Marriage: $8.00 (from 1853)
Divorce: $8.00 (from 1853)

Washington
Washington Department of Health

Center for Health Statistics
P.O. Box 9709
Olympia, WA 98507-9709
(360) 753-5936
(360) 753-4379 (credit card
    may be used with service
    fee)
Fax: (360)-352-2586
Birth: $13.00 (from 1907)
Death: $13.00 (from 1907)
Marriage: $13.00 (from 1968)
Divorce: $13.00 (from 1968)

West Virginia
West Virginia Division of Vital
    Statistics
Capitol Complex, Building Three,
    Room 516
Charleston, WV 25305
(304) 558-2931 (credit card
    charges at same number)
Birth: $5.00 (from 1917; some
    available from 1800 to 1917)
Death: $5.00 (from 1917; some
    available from 1800 to 1917)
Marriage: $5.00 (from 1964;
    indexes from 1921 to 1963)
Divorce: County records (indexes
    from 1967)

Wisconsin
Wisconsin Section of Vital
    Statistics
P.O. Box 309
Madison, WI 53701
(608) 266-1371
(608) 266-1372
Birth: $12.00 (from 1870)
Death: $7.00 (from 1870)
Marriage: $7.00 (from 1870)
Divorce: $7.00 (from 1907)

Wyoming
Wyoming Vital Records
Hathaway Building
Cheyenne, WY 82002
(307) 777-7591
Birth: $12.00 (from 1909)
Death: $9.00 (from 1909)
Marriage: $12.00 (from 1941)
Divorce: $12.00 (from 1941)

State Archives and Other Resource Centers

Following are the names and addresses of state archives (the first listing under each state name) and other resource centers that may be useful to you in your search for your African-American forebears. Check with your local or county librarian to identify local or regional research facilities that may have holdings appropriate to your research activities.

Alabama
Alabama Department of Archives
   and History
624 Washington Avenue
Montgomery, AL 36130-0100
(334) 242-4435

Alabama Genealogical Society, Inc.
   (AGS)
Special Collection Department
800 Lakeshore Drive
Birmingham, AL 35229
(205) 475-5261

Southern Society of Genealogists,
   Inc.
Stewart University
P.O. Box 295
Centre, AL 35960
(205) 475-5261

Alaska
Division of Libraries and Archives
Department of Education
P.O. Box 110571
Juneau, AK 99811
(907) 465-2270

University of Alaska, Anchorage
Consortium Library
Archives and Manuscript
  Department
3211 Providence Drive
Anchorage, AK 99508
(907) 786-1848

University of Alaska, Fairbanks
E. E. Rasmuson Library
Rare Books, Archives and
  Manuscripts
Fairbanks, AK 99701
(907) 474-7481

Arizona
Arizona State Genealogy Library
Department of Library, Archives,
  and Public Records
State Capitol
1700 West Washington
Phoenix, AZ 85007
(602) 542-3942

Arizona Society of Genealogists
6565 East Grant Road
Tuscon, AZ 85715

Arizona State Genealogical
  Society
P.O. Box 42075
Tuscon, AZ 85733-2075

Arkansas
Arkansas History Commission
  and State Archives
1 Capitol Mall
Little Rock, AR 72201
(501) 682-6900

Arkansas Genealogical Society
P.O. Box 908
Hot Springs, AR 71902-0908
(501) 262-4513

California
California State Archives
Division of the Secretary of State's
  Office
1020 "O" Street
Sacramento, CA 95814
(916) 773-3000

California Historical Society
2909 Pacific Avenue
San Francisco, CA 94109
(415) 567-1848

California Genealogical Society
300 Brannan Street
P.O. Box 77105
San Francisco, CA 94107-0105
(415) 777-9936

Southern California Genealogical
  Society
P.O. Box 4377
Burbank, CA 91503
(818) 843-7247

California Afro-American Museum
600 State Drive
Los Angeles, CA 90052
(213) 744-7432

Colorado
Division of Archives and Public
  Records
Department of Administration

1313 Sherman Street
Room 1B-20
Denver, CO 80203
(303) 866-2055

Colorado Genealogical
    Society
10 West Fourteenth Avenue
    Parkway
Denver, CO 80204
(303) 640-6200

Black American West Museum
    and Heritage Center
3091 California Street
Denver, CO 80204
(303) 292-2566

Connecticut
Conneticut State Library
History and Genealogy
    Unit
231 Capitol Avenue
Hartford, CT 06106

The Stamford Historical
    Society
1508 High Ridge Road
Stamford, CT 06903
(203) 329-1183

Connecticut Society of
    Genealogists, Inc.
175 Maple Street
East Hartford

Mailing Address:
P.O. Box 435
Glastonbury, CT 06083-0435
(203) 569-0002

Delaware
Division of Historical and Cultural
    Affairs
Hall of Records
Dover, DE 19901
(302) 739-5318

Historical Society of Delaware
505 Market Street Mall
Wilmington, DE 19801
(302) 655-7161

Delaware Genealogical Society
505 Market Street Mall
Wilmington, DE 19801
(302) 655-7161

Florida
Florida State Archives
Bureau of Archives and Records
    Management
Division of Library and
    Information Services
Public Services Section
R.A. Gray Building
500 South Bronough Street
Tallahassee, FL 32399-0250
(904) 487-2073

Florida State Genealogical
    Society
P.O. Box 102496
Tallahassee, FL 32302-2249
(305) 375-5580

Georgia
Georgia Department of Archives
    and History
330 Capital Avenue SE

Atlanta, GA 30334
(404) 656-2350

Georgia Genealogical Society
P.O. Box 54575
Atlanta, GA 30308-0575
(404) 475-4404

Hawaii
Hawaii State Archives
Department of Accounting
   and General Services
Iolani Palace Grounds
Honolulu, HI 96813
(808) 586-0329

Hawaiian Historical Society
560 Kawaiahao Street
Honolulu, HI 96813
(808) 537-6271

Genealogical Resource Center
Alu Like
Native Hawaiian Libraries Project
1025 Mapunapuna Street
Honolulu, HI 96819-8940
(808) 535-6750

Idaho
The Idaho State Historical Society
Library and Archives
450 North Fourth Street
Boise, ID 83702
(208) 334-3356

The Idaho Genealogical Society,
   Inc.
325 West State Street
Boise, ID 83705-2867
(208) 384-0542

Illinois
Illinois State Archives Division
Office of the Secretary of State
Archives Building
Capitol Complex
Springfield, IL 62791
(217) 782-4682

Illinois State Genealogical Society
P.O. Box 10495
Springfield, IL 62756
(217) 789-1968

Chicago Genealogical Society
P.O. Box 1160
Chicago, IL 60690
(312) 725-1306

Du Sable Museum of African-
   American History and Art
740 East Fifty-Sixth Place
Chicago, IL 60690
(312) 947-0600

African American Cultural
   and Genealogical Society
314 North Main Street
Decatur, IL 62523
(217) 429-7458

Indiana
Indiana State Library
William Henry Smith Memorial
   Library
140 North Senate Avenue
Indianapolis, IN 46204
(317) 232-3373

Indiana Historical Society
315 West Ohio Street

Indianapolis, IN 46202
(317) 232-1882

Indiana State Museum: Freetown
  Village
202 North Alabama Street
Indianapolis, IN 46206
(317) 232-1637

Iowa
State Historical Society of Iowa
Library and Iowa State Archives
600 East Locust
Des Moines, IA 50319
(515) 281-5111

Iowa Genealogical Society
6000 Douglas
P.O. Box 7735
Des Moines, IA 50322-7735
(515) 276-0287

Kansas
Kansas State Historical Society
Archives Division
Memorial Building
Reference Services
120 West Tenth Street
Topeka, KS 66612
(913) 296-4774

Kansas Genealogical Research
Village Square Mall
P.O. Box 103
Dodge City, KS 67801
(316) 225-1951

The Black Archives of
  MidAmerica
2033 Vine Street

Kansas City, Kansas 66106
(816) 483-1300

Kentucky
Kentucky Department for Library
  and Archives
Public Records Division
300 Coffee Tree Road, First Floor
P.O. Box 537
Frankfort, KY 40602-0537
(502) 564-8704

Kentucky Historical Society
P.O. Box 1792
Frankfort, KY 40602
(502) 564-3016

Kentucky Genealogical
  Society
P.O. Box 153
Frankfort, KY 40602
(502) 223-0492

Louisiana
Office of the Secretary of State
Division of Archives
3851 Essen Lane
P.O. Box 94125
Baton Rouge, LA 70804-9125
(504) 922-1206

Louisiana Genealogical and
  Historical Society
P.O. Box 3454
Baton Rouge, LA 70821
(504) 766-3018

Maine
Maine State Archives
State House Station #84

Augusta, ME 04333-0084
(207) 287-5790

Maine Historical Society
485 Congress Street
Portland, ME 04101
(207) 774-1822

Maryland
Maryland State Archives
Hall of Records Building
350 Rowe Boulevard
Annapolis, MD 21401
(410) 974-3914
(410) 974-3916

Maryland Genealogical Society
201 West Monument Street
Baltimore, MD 21201
(410) 685-3750

Banneker-Douglass Museum
84 Franklin Street
Annapolis, MD 21401
(301) 974-3955

Massachusetts
Archives of the
    Commonwealth
Reference Desk
220 Morrissey Boulevard
Boston, MA 02125
(617) 727-2816
(617) 727-8730

Massachusetts Historical
    Society
1154 Boylston Street
Boston, MA 02215
(617) 536-1608

Massachusetts Genealogical
    Council
c/o New England Historic
    Genealogical Society
101 Newbury Street
Boston, MA 02116-3007
(617) 536-5740

New England Historic
    Genealogical Society
101 Newbury Street
Boston, MA 02116-3007
(617) 536-5740

Michigan
State Archives of Michigan
717 West Allegan
Lansing, MI 48918
(517) 373-1408

Library of Michigan
P.O. Box 30007
Lansing, MI 48909
(517) 373-1300

Museum of African-American
    History
Federick Douglass Street
Detroit, Michigan 48202
(313) 833-9800

Minnesota
Minnesota Historical Society
Research Center
345 Kellog Boulevard West
St. Paul, MN 55102
(612) 296-6980

Minnesota Genealogical Society
1650 Carol Avenue

P.O. Box 16069
St. Paul, MN 55116-0069
(612) 645-3671

Mississippi
Mississippi Department of
Archives and History
P.O. Box 571
Jackson, MS 39205-0571
(601) 359-6876

Missouri
Missouri State Archives
600 West Main
P.O. Box 788
Jefferson City, MO 65102
(314) 751-3280

Missouri State Genealogical
Association
P.O. Box 833
Columbia, MO 65205-0833
(816) 747-9330

Heart of America Genealogical
Society
c/o Public Library
311 East Twelfth Street
Kansas City, MO 64106
(816) 221-2685

Montana
Montana Historical Society
Memorial Building
225 North Roberts Street
Helena, MT 59620
(406) 444-2681

Missoula Public Library
301 East Main

Missoula, MT 59802-4799
(406) 721-2665

Montana Historical Society
Foundation
P.O. Box 863
Helena, MT 59624
(406) 449-3770

Yellowstone Genealogy Forum
c/o Parmly Billings Library
510 North Broadway
Billings, MT 59101
(406) 657-8257

Nebraska
State Archives Division
Nebraska State Historical Society
Division of Reference Services
1500 "R" Street
P.O. Box 82554
Lincoln, NE 68501-2554
(402) 471-4771

Nebraska State Genealogical
Society
P.O. Box 5608
Lincoln, NE 68505-0608
(402) 266-8881

Great Plains Black Museum
22213 Lake Street
Omaha, Nebraska 68110
(402) 345-2212

Nevada
Nevada State Library and Archives
Division of Archives and Records
100 Steward Street
Carson City, NV 89710-4285
(702) 687-5210

Nevada Historical Society
1650 North Virginia Street
Reno, NV 89503
(702) 688-1191

Northeastern Nevada Genealogical
    Society
P.O. Box 2550
Elko, NV 89801
(702) 738-3418

New Hampshire
New Hampshire Division of
    Records Management and
    Department of State
71 South Fruit Street
Concord, NH 03301-2410
(603) 271-2236

New Jersey
Department of State
Division of Archives and Records
    Management
Bureau of Archives and Records
    Preservation
State Library Building
State Department of Education
185 West State Street, CN307
Trenton, NJ 08625-0307
(609) 292-6260

Newark Public Library
5 Washington Street
Newark, NJ 07101
(973) 733-7820

Genealogy Club of the Library
    of the New Jersey Historical
    Society
230 Broadway

Newark, NJ 07104
(973) 483-3939

New Mexico
New Mexico Records Center
    and Archives
404 Montezuma Street
Santa Fe, NM 87501
(505) 827-7332

New Mexico Genealogical Society
P.O. Box 8283
Albuquerque, NM 87198-8283
(505) 281-3133
(505) 255-6116

New York
New York State Archives
New York Department of Education
Cultural Education Center
    No. 11D40
Empire State Plaza
Albany, NY 12230
(518) 474-8955

New York Genealogical and
    Biographical Society
122–126 East Fifty-Eighth Street
New York, NY 10022-1939
(212) 755-8532

New York State Historical
    Association
P.O. Box 800
Cooperstown, NY 13326
(607) 547-2509

New York Public Library
Schomberg Center for Research
    in Black Culture

515 Malcolm X Boulevard
New York, NY 10037
(212) 491-2200

The Brooklyn Historical Society
128 Pierrepont Street
Brooklyn, NY 11201
(718) 624-0890

North Carolina
North Carolina State Archives
Department of Cultural Resources
Division of Archives and History
109 East Jones Street
Raleigh, NC 27601-2807
(919) 733-3952

North Carolina Genealogical Society
P.O. Box 1492
Raleigh, NC 27602
(919) 733-3991

North Dakota
State Archives and Historical
   Research Library
Heritage Center
612 East Boulevard Avenue
Bismark, ND 58505-0830
(701) 224-2668

State Historical Society of North
   Dakota
Heritage Center
612 East Boulevard Avenue
Bismark, ND 58505-0830
(701) 224-2668

Ohio
Ohio Historical Society
Archives Library Division

1982 Velma Avenue
Columbus, OH 43211
(614) 297-2300

State Library of Ohio
65 South Front Street
Columbus, OH 43266-0334
(614) 644-6966

African-American Museum
1765 Crawford Road
Cleveland, Ohio 44101
(216) 791-1700

National Afro-American Museum
   and Cultural Center
Bush Row Road
Wilberforce, Ohio 45384
(513) 376-6011

Oklahoma
Oklahoma Department of Libraries
Archives Division
200 NE Eighteenth Street
Oklahoma City, OK 73105
800-522-8116

Oklahoma State Historical Society
Library Resources Division
Wiley Post Historical Building
2100 North Lincoln Boulevard
Oklahoma City, OK 73105
(405) 521-2491

Oregon
Archives Division
Secretary of State
800 Summer Street NE
Salem, OR 97310
(503) 373-0701

Oregon Genealogical Society
223 North "A" Street,
  Springfield, OR
P.O. Box 10306
Eugene, OR 97440-2306
(514) 746-7924

Genealogical Heritage Council
  of Oregon
Douglas County Court House
Room 111
P.O. Box 579
Roseburg, OR 97201
(541) 672-3311, ext. 6178

Pennsylvania
Pennsylvania State Archives
Reference Section
Third and Forster Streets
P.O. Box 1026
Harrisburg, PA 17108-1026
(717) 783-3281

Afro-American Genealogy
  Group
P.O. Box 1798
Philadelphia, PA 19105-1798
(215) 572-6063

Genealogical Society of
  Pennsylvania
1300 Locust Street
Philadelphia, PA 19107-5699
(215) 545-0391

Historical Society of
  Pennsylvania
1300 Locust Street
Philadelphia, PA 19107-5699
(215) 732-6200

Rhode Island
Rhode Island State Archives
337 Westminster Street
Providence, RI 02903
(401) 277-2353

Rhode Island Black Heritage Society
1 Hilton Street
Providence, Rhode Island 02903
(401) 751-3490

South Carolina
South Carolina Department of
  Archives and History
1430 Senate Street
Columbia, SC 29211-1669
(803) 734-8577

South Carolina Historical Society
100 Meeting Street
Charleston, SC 29401
(803) 723-3225

Avery Research Center for African-
  American History and Culture
67 George Street
Charleston, South Carolina 29401
(803) 792-5742

South Dakota
South Dakota Archives
Cultural Heritage Center
900 Governors Drive
Pierre, SD 57501-2217
(605) 773-3804

State Historical Society
900 Governors Drive
Pierre, SD 57501-2217
(605) 773-3458

Tennessee
Tenneessee State Library and
  Archives Building
403 Seventh Avenue North
Nashville, TN 37243-0312
(615) 741-2764

Afro-American Museum
730 Martin Luther King Jr.
  Boulevard
Chattanooga, TN 37402
(615) 267-1076

Tennessee Genealogical Society
3340 Poplar Avenue,
  Suite 327
Memphis, TN 38111
(901) 327-3273

Texas
Texas State Library and Archives
  Division
1201 Barzos Street
Box 12927, Capitol Station
Austin, TX 78711
(512) 463-5480

Texas State Genealogical
  Society
3219 Meadow Oaks Drive
Temple, TX 76502-1752
(817) 778-2073

Utah
State Archives and Record
  Services
Archives Building
State Capitol
Salt Lake City, UT 84114
(801) 538-3013

Utah Genealogist Association
P.O. Box 1144
Salt Lake City, UT 84110
(801) 262-7263
(801) 531-2091

Church of Jesus Christ
  of Latter-day Saints
Family History Library
35 North West Temple
Salt Lake City, UT 84150
(801) 240-2331

Vermont
Vermont Historical Society
  Library and Museum
Pavilion Office Building
109 State Street
Montpelier, VT 05609
(802) 828-2291

Genealogical Society of Vermont
Main Street
P.O. Box 422
Pittsford, VT 05763
(802) 483-2957
(802) 483-2900

Virginia
Virginia State Libraries and
  Archives
Eleventh Street at Capitol
  Square
Richmond, VA 23219-3419
(804) 692-3888

Virginia Historical Society
P.O. Box 7311
Richmond, VA 23221-0311
(804) 358-4901

Virginia Genealogical Society
P.O. Box 7469
Richmond, VA 23221
(804) 285-8954

Washington
Division of Archives
Office of the Secretary of State
Washington State Archives and
    Records Center Building
1120 Washington Street SE
Olympia, WA 98504-0238
(206) 586-1492

Washington State Genealogical
    Society
P.O. Box 1422
Olympia, WA 98507
(206) 352-0595

West Virginia
Division of Archives and History
Science and Culture Center
    Capitol Complex
1900 Kanawha Boulevard East
Charleston, WV 25305-0300
(304) 558-0220

West Virginia Historical Society
Cultural Center

1900 Kanewha Boulevard
    East
Charleston, WV 25305-0300
(304) 558-0220

Wisconsin
State Historical Society
    of Wisconsin
Archives Division
816 State Street
Madison, WI 53706
(608) 264-6536

Wisconsin State Genealogical
    Society
2109 Twentieth Avenue
Monroe, WI 53566
(608) 325-2609

Wyoming
Wyoming State Archives
Research Division
6101 Yellowstone Road
Cheyenne, WY 82002
(307) 777-7016

Laramie County Library
2900 Central Avenue
Cheyenne, WY 82001
(307) 634-3561

Appendix III

National Archives and Records Administration: Regional Branches

There are seventeen National Archives regional branches located throughout the United States. You can initiate research in any of these facilities in person or by telephone, mail, fax, or E-mail. There are also two locations for national personnel records: civilian and military. These can be reached by mail, E-mail, or fax.

Anchorage
  (Pacific Alaska Region)
654 West Third Avenue
Anchorage, AK 99501-2145
Telephone: (907) 271-2443
E-mail: archives@alaska.nara.gov
Fax: (907) 271-2442
Area served: Alaska

Atlanta
  (East Point)
  (Southeast Region)
1557 St. Joseph Avenue
East Point, GA 30344-2593
Telephone: (404) 763-7477
E-mail: archives@atlanta.nara.gov
Fax: (404) 763-7033

Area served: Alabama, Florida, Georgia, Kentucky, Mississippi, North Carolina, South Carolina, Tennessee

Boston (Waltham)
  (Northeast Region)
380 Trapelo Road
Waltham, MA 02154-6399
Telephone: (781) 647-8100
E-mail: archives@waltham.nara.gov
Fax: (781) 647-8460
Area served: Connecticut, Maine, Massachusetts, New Hampshire, Rhode Island, Vermont

Chicago (Great Lakes Region)
7358 South Pulaski Road
Chicago, IL 60629-5898
Telephone: (773) 581-1294
E-mail: archives@chicago.nara.gov
Fax: (312) 353-1294
Area served: Illinois, Indiana,
Michigan, Minnesota, Ohio,
Wisconsin

Dayton (Great Lakes Region)
3150 Springboro Road
Dayton, OH 45439-1883
Telephone: (937) 225-2852
E-mail: center@dayton.nara.gov
Fax: (937) 225-7236
Area served: Indiana, Michigan,
Minnesota, Ohio

Denver (Rocky Mountain Region)
Building 48, Denver Federal
Center
Denver, CO 80225
P.O. Box 25307
Denver, CO 80225-0307
Telephone: (303) 236-0804
E-mail: center@denver.nara.gov
Fax: (303) 236-9297
Area served: Colorado, Montana,
New Mexico, North Dakota,
South Dakota, Utah, Wyoming

Fort Worth (Southwest Region)
501 West Felix Street, Building 1
Fort Worth, TX 76115-3405
P.O. Box 6216
Fort Worth, TX 76115-0216
Telephone: (817) 334-5525
E-mail: archives@ftworth.nara.gov
Fax: (817) 334-5621

Area served: Arkansas, Louisiana,
Oklahoma, Texas

Kansas City (Central Plains
Region)
2312 East Bannister Road
Kansas City, MO 64131-3011
Telephone: (816) 926-6272
E-mail: archives@Kansascity.nara.
gov
Fax: (816) 926-6982
Area served: Iowa, Kansas,
Missouri, Nebraska

Laguna Niguel, California
(Pacific Region)
24000 Avila Road
First Floor, East Entrance
Laguna Niguel, CA 92677-3497
P.O. Box 6719
Laguna Niguel, CA 92607-6719
Telephone: (714) 360-2641
E-mail: center@laguna.nara.gov
Fax: (714) 360-2624
Area served: Arizona, southern
California, Clark County,
Nevada

Lee's Summit, Missouri (Central
Plains Region)
200 Space Center Drive
Lee's Summit, Missouri
64064-1182
Telephone: (816) 478-7079
E-mail: center@kansascity.nara.gov
Fax: (816) 478-7625
Area served: New Jersey, New
York, Puerto Rico and the U.S.
Virgin Islands (temporary
records). *Temporary records*

refers to the Virgin Islands location. The New York City center maintains permanent records on the Virgin Islands.

New York City (Northeast Region)
201 Varick Street
New York, NY 10014-4811
Telephone: (212) 337-1300
E-mail: archives@newyork.nara.gov
Fax: (212) 337-1306
Area served: New Jersey, New York, Puerto Rico, U.S. Virgin Islands

Philadelphia (Center City)
(Midatlantic Region)
Ninth and Market Streets
Philadelphia, PA 19107-4292
Telephone: (215) 597-3000
E-mail: archives@philarch.nara.gov
Fax: (215) 597-2303
Area served: Delaware, Maryland, Pennsylvania, Virginia, West Virginia

Philadelphia (Northeast)
(Midatlantic Region)
14700 Townsend Road
Philadelphia, PA 19154-1096
Telephone: (215) 671-9027
E-mail: center@philadelphia.nara.gov
Fax: (215) 671-9027
Area served: Delaware, Pennsylvania, federal courts in Maryland, Virginia, and West Virginia

Pittsfield, Massachusetts
(Northeast Region)
10 Conte Drive
Pittsfield, MA 01201-8230
Telephone: (413) 445-6885
E-mail: archives@pittsfield.nara.gov
Fax: (413) 445-7599

San Francisco
(Pacific Region)
1000 Commodore Drive
San Bruno, CA 94066-2350
Telephone: (650) 876-9009
E-mail: center@sanbruno.nara.gov
Fax: (650) 876-9233
Area served: Northern California, Guam, Hawaii, Nevada (except Clark County), American Samoa, Trust Territory of the Pacific Islands

Seattle (Pacific Alaska Region)
6125 Sand Point Way NE
Seattle, WA 98115-7999
Telephone: (206) 526-6507
E-mail: archives@seattle.nara.gov
Fax: (206) 526-4344
Area served: Idaho, Oregon, Washington

St. Louis (National Personnel Records Center)
Civilian Personnel Records
111 Winnebago Street
St. Louis, MO 63118-4199
E-mail: center@cpr.nara.gov
Fax: (314) 425-5719

National Personnel Records Center
Military Personnel Records
9700 Page Avenue
St. Louis, MO 63132-5100
E-mail: center@stlouis.nara.gov
Fax: (314) 538-4005

Suitland, Maryland (Washington
National Records Center)

4205 Suitland Road
Suitland, MD 20746-8001
Telephone: (301) 457-7000
E-mail: center@suitland.nara.
  gov
Fax: 301-457-7117
Area served: Washington, D.C.,
  area, Maryland, Virginia, West
  Virginia

Appendix IV
Federal Census Forms

1790 CENSUS — UNITED STATES

Call No. _____

State _____

County	City	Page	Head of Family	Free White Males		Free White Females	All Other Persons	Slaves
				16 & up incl. head of families	Under 16	Incl. head of family		

1800–1810 CENSUS — UNITED STATES

Call No. _____

State _____ County _____ City _____

Head of Family	Free White Males					Free White Females					All Others	Slaves	Remarks
	Under 10	10–16	16–26	26–45	45 & Over	Under 10	10–16	16–26	26–45	45 & Over			

Page _____

1820 CENSUS — UNITED STATES

Call No. _____

State _____ County _____ City _____

Head of Family	Free White Males						Free White Females					Foreigners not naturalized	Agriculture	Commerce	Manufactures	Free Colored	Slaves	Remarks
	Under 10	10–16	16–18	16–26	26–45	45 and over	Under 10	10–16	16–26	26–45	45 and over							

Page _____

Federal Census Forms 233

1830-1840 CENSUS – UNITED STATES

STATE | COUNTY | CITY | CALL NUMBER

HEAD OF FAMILY | Page

FREE WHITE MALES: Under 5, 5-10, 10-15, 15-20, 20-30, 30-40, 40-50, 50-60, 60-70, 70-80, 80-90, 90-100, Over 100

FREE WHITE FEMALES: Under 5, 5-10, 10-15, 15-20, 20-30, 30-40, 40-50, 50-60, 60-70, 70-80, 80-90, 90-100, Over 100

Slaves | Free Colored | Foreigners Not Naturalized

1850 CENSUS – UNITED STATES

STATE | COUNTY | TOWN/TOWNSHIP | CALL NUMBER

Page | Dwelling Number | Family Number | NAMES | Age | Sex | Color | OCCUPATION, ETC. | Value—Real Estate | BIRTHPLACE | Married Within Year | School Within Year | Can't Read or Write | Enumeration Date | REMARKS

1860 CENSUS – UNITED STATES

STATE   COUNTY   TOWN/TOWNSHIP   P.O.   CALL NUMBER

Page	Dwelling No.	Family No.	NAMES	Age	Sex	Color	OCCUPATION, ETC.	Value—Real Estate	Value—Personal Property	BIRTHPLACE	Married in Year	School in Year	Can't Read or Write	Enumeration Date	REMARKS

1870 CENSUS – UNITED STATES

STATE   COUNTY   TOWN/TOWNSHIP   P.O.   CALL NUMBER

Page	Dwelling No.	Family No.	NAMES	Age	Sex	Color	OCCUPATION, ETC.	Value—Real Estate	Value—Personal Prop.	BIRTHPLACE	Father Foreign Born	Mother Foreign Born	Month Born in Year	Month Married in Year	School in Year	Can't Read or Write	Eligible To Vote	Date of Enumeration

1880 CENSUS – UNITED STATES

STATE COUNTY TOWN/TOWNSHIP CALL NUMBER

Page
Dwelling Number
Family Number

NAMES

Color
Sex
Age Prior to June 1st
Month of Birth if Born in Census Year
Relationship to Head of House
Single
Married
Widowed
Divorced
Married in Census Year
Occupation
Miscellaneous Information
Cannot Read or Write
Place of Birth
Place of Birth of Father
Place of Birth of Mother
Date Enumeration

1900 CENSUS – UNITED STATES

MICROFILM ROLL NUMBER
STATE COUNTY
TOWN/TOWNSHIP CALL NUMBER
SUPV. DIST. NO. ENUM. DIST. NO. DATE
SHEET NUMBER PAGE NUMBER

LOCATION
Street
House Number
Dwelling Number
Family Number

NAME
of each person whose place of abode on June 1, 1900, was in this family

Relation to head of family

PERSONAL DESCRIPTION
Color
Sex
Month of birth
Year of birth
Age
Single, married, widowed, divorced
Number of years married
Mother of how many children
Number of these children living

NATIVITY
Place of birth
Place of birth of father
Place of birth of mother

CITIZENSHIP
Year of immigration to United States
No. of years in U.S.
Naturalization

OCCUPATION
Type
Number of months not employed

EDUCATION
Attended school (months)
Can read
Can write
Can speak English

Home owned or rented
Home owned free or mortgaged
Farm or house

1910 CENSUS – UNITED STATES

STATE	COUNTY	TOWN/TOWNSHIP	ENUM. DIST. NO.	PAGE NO.

LOCATION				NAME	PERSONAL DESCRIPTION								NATIVITY		
STREET NAME	HOUSE NUMBER	VISITATION NUMBER	FAMILY NUMBER	OF EACH PERSON WHOSE PLACE OF ABODE ON APRIL 15, 1910, WAS IN THIS FAMILY	RELATION TO HEAD OF HOUSE	SEX	RACE	AGE	SINGLE/MARRIED/ WIDOWED/DIVORCED	NUMBER OF YEARS PRESENT MARRIAGE	NO. OF CHILDREN BORN THIS MOTHER	NUMBER OF THESE CHILDREN LIVING	PLACE OF BIRTH OF THIS PERSON	PLACE OF BIRTH OF FATHER	PLACE OF BIRTH OF MOTHER

FRONT

1910 CENSUS – UNITED STATES (CONTINUED)

STATE	COUNTY	TOWN/TOWNSHIP	ENUM. DIST. NO.	PAGE NO.

NAME	CITIZENSHIP			OCCUPATION					EDUCATION			HOME OWNERSHIP							
OF EACH PERSON WHOSE PLACE OF ABODE ON APRIL 15, 1910, WAS IN THIS FAMILY (FROM OTHER SIDE OF THIS FORM)	YEAR OF IMMIGRATION TO U.S.	NATURALIZED/ALIEN	NATIVE LANGUAGE	TRADE OR PROFESSION	NATURE OF BUSINESS	EMPLOYER/EMPLOYEE/ SELF-EMPLOYED	IF EMPLOYEE EMPLOYED/ UNEMPLOYED	IF EMPLOYEE WEEKS OUT OF WORK IN 1909	ABLE TO READ	ABLE TO WRITE	ATTENDED SCHOOL SINCE SEPT. 1, 1909	OWNED/RENTED	OWNED FREE/ MORTGAGED	FARM/HOUSE	NO. OF FARM SCHEDULE	UNION/CONFEDERATE VETERAN	BLIND	DEAF AND DUMB

BACK

1920 CENSUS — UNITED STATES

STATE		SUPERVISOR'S DISTRICT #	SHEET
COUNTY		ENUMERATION DISTRICT #	NO.

NAME OF INCORPORATED PLACE

TOWNSHIP OR OTHER COUNTY DIVISION

WARD OF CITY

NAME OF INSTITUTION

ENUMERATED BY ME ON THE ____ DAY OF ____, 1920

ENUMERATOR

PLACE OF ABODE				NAME	RELATION	TENURE		PERSONAL DESCRIPTION				CITIZENSHIP			EDUCATION		
STREET, AVENUE, ETC.	HOUSE NUMBER OR FARM	NUMBER OF DWELLING HOUSE (VISITATION ORDER)	NUMBER OF FAMILY (VISITATION ORDER)	OF EACH PERSON WHOSE PLACE OF ABODE ON JANUARY 1, 1920, WAS IN THIS FAMILY	RELATIONSHIP TO HEAD OF HOUSEHOLD	HOME OWNED OR RENTED	IF OWNED, FREE OR MORTGAGED	SEX	COLOR OR RACE	AGE AT LAST BIRTHDAY	SINGLE, MARRIED WIDOWED, OR DIVORCED	YEAR OF IMMIGRATION TO U.S.	NATURALIZED OR ALIEN	IF NATURALIZED, YEAR OF NATURALIZATION	ATTENDED SCHOOL ANYTIME SINCE SEPT. 1, 1919	ABLE TO READ	ABLE TO WRITE
1	2	3	4	5	6	7	8	9	10	11	12	13	14	15	16	17	18

FRONT

STATE		SUPERVISOR'S DISTRICT #		SHEET NO.
COUNTY		ENUMERATION DISTRICT #		
TOWNSHIP OR OTHER COUNTY DIVISION	NAME OF INCORPORATED PLACE		WARD OF CITY	
NAME OF INSTITUTION	ENUMERATED BY ME ON THE ___ DAY OF ___, 1920		ENUMERATOR	

1920 CENSUS — UNITED STATES

NAME	NATIVITY AND MOTHER TONGUE								OCCUPATION			
OF EACH PERSON WHOSE PLACE OF ABODE ON JANUARY 1, 1920, WAS IN THIS FAMILY (from other side of form).	PLACE OF BIRTH OF EACH PERSON AND PARENTS OF EACH PERSON ENUMERATED. IF BORN IN U.S., GIVE STATE OR TERRITORY. IF FOREIGN BIRTH, GIVE THE PLACE OF BIRTH, AND, IN ADDITION, THE MOTHER TONGUE.						ABLE TO SPEAK ENGLISH	TRADE, PROFESSION, OR PARTICULAR KIND OF WORK DONE.	INDUSTRY, BUSINESS, OR ESTABLISHMENT IN WHICH AT WORK.	EMPLOYER, SALARY OR WAGE WORKER, OR WORKING ON OWN ACCOUNT.	NUMBER OF FARM SCHEDULE
	PERSON		FATHER		MOTHER						
	PLACE OF BIRTH	MOTHER TONGUE	PLACE OF BIRTH	MOTHER TONGUE	PLACE OF BIRTH	MOTHER TONGUE					
5	19	20	21	22	23	24	25	26	27	28	29

BACK

Bibliography

Andereck, Paul A., and Richard A. Pence. *Computer Genealogy: A Guide to Research Through High Technology.* Salt Lake City: Ancestry Publishing Incorporated, 1985.

Ball, Edward. *Slaves in the Family.* New York: Farrar, Straus & Giroux, 1998.

Bentley, Elizabeth Petty. *County Courthouse Book,* 2nd ed. Baltimore: Genealogical Publishing Co., Inc., 1995.

Bergman, Peter M. *The Chronological History of the Negro in America.* New York, Evanston, Ill., and London: Harper & Row, 1969.

Blockson, Charles L., with Ron Fry. *Black Genealogy.* Englewood Cliffs, N.J.: Prentice Hall, 1977.

Bogger, Tommy L. *Free Blacks in Norfolk, Virginia, 1790–1860: The Darker Side of Freedom.* Charlottesville: University Press of Virginia, 1997.

Bowen, Catherine Drinker. *Miracle at Philadelphia: The Story of the Constitutional Convention May to September 1787.* Boston: Little, Brown, 1966.

Burnside, Madeline, and Rosemarie Robotham. *Spirits of the Passage: The Transatlantic Slave Trade in the Seventeenth Century.* New York: Simon & Schuster Editions, 1997.

Brunner, Borgna, ed. *Information Please Almanac.* Boston: Information Please LLC, 1997–.

Byers, Paula K., ed. *African American Genealogical Source Book.* New York: Gale Research, Inc., 1995.

Cantor, George. *Historic Landmarks of Black America.* Detroit and London: Gale Research, Inc., 1991.

Chitwood, Oliver Perry, and Frank Lawrence Owsley. *A Short History of the American People,* 2nd ed. Princeton, N.J.: D. Van Nostrand Company, Inc., 1955.

Chuks-orgi, Ogonna. *Names From Africa: Their Origin, Meaning, and Pronunciation.* Chicago: Johnson Publishing Company, Inc., 1972.

Croom, Emily Ann. *The Genealogist's Companion & Sourcebook.* Cincinnati: Betterway Books, 1994.

_____. *Unpuzzling Your Past: A Basic Guide to Genealogy,* 3rd ed. Cincinnati: Betterway Books, 1995.

Doane, Gilbert H., and James B. Bell. *Searching for Your Ancestors: The How and Why of Genealogy,* 6th ed. Minneapolis and London: University of Minnesota Press, 1994.

Fletcher, Marvin. *The Black Soldier and Officer in the United States Army, 1891–1917.* Columbia: University of Missouri Press, 1974.

Fowler, Arlen L. *Black Infantry in the West 1869–1891.* Westport, Connecticut: Greenwood Publishing Corp., 1971.

Franklin, John Hope, and Alfred A. Moss Jr. *From Slavery to Freedom,* 7th ed. New York: McGraw-Hill, 1994.

Garland, Penn I. *The Afro-American Press and Its Editors.* New York: Arno Press, 1969.

Genovese, Eugene D. *Roll Jordan, Roll: The World the Slaves Made.* New York: Pantheon Books, 1974.

Goode, Kenneth G. *California's Black Pioneers: A Brief Historical Survey.* Santa Barbara: McNally and Loftin, 1974.

Greenwood, Val D. *The Researcher's Guide to American Genealogy,* 2nd ed. Baltimore: Genealogical Publishing Co., Inc., 1990.

Hinshaw, William Wade. *Encyclopedia of American Quaker Genealogy.* Baltimore: Genealogical Publishing Co., 1969.

Hornsby, Alton Jr. *Chronology of African-American History: Significant Events and People From 1619 to the Present.* Detroit, Washington, D.C., and London: Gale Research, Inc., 1991.

Katz, William L. *Eyewitness: The Negro in American History.* New York, Toronto, and London: Pitman Publishing Corporation, 1967.

_____. *The Black West,* rev. ed. Garden City, N.J.: Anchor Press/Doubleday, 1973.

Kirkham, Kay E. *How to Read the Handwriting and Records of Early America.* Salt Lake City, Utah: Kay Publishing Co., 1961.

Koger, Larry. *Black Slaveowners: Free Black Slave Masters in South Carolina, 1790–1860.* Columbia: University of South Carolina Press, 1994.

Larrie, Reginald, R. *Makin' Free: African-Americans in the Northwest Territory.* Detroit: B Ethridge Books, 1981.

Leckie, William H. *The Buffalo Soldiers: A Narrative of the Negro Cavalry in the West.* Norman: University of Oklahoma Press, 1967.

McPherson, James M. *The Negro's Civil War: How Blacks Felt and Acted During the War for the Union.* New York: Ballantine Books, 1991.

Mitros, David, comp. *Slave Records of Morris County, New Jersey 1756–1841.* Morris County: Morris County Heritage Commission, 1991.

Morris, Richard B., ed. *Encyclopedia of American History: Bicentennial Edition.* New York: Harper & Row, 1976.

Morris, Thomas D. *Southern Slavery and the Law: 1619–1860.* Chapel Hill: The University of North Carolina Press, 1996.

National Archives and Records Service. *Guide to Genealogical Research in the National Archives.* Washington, D.C., 1982.

Neagles, James C. *The Library of Congress: A Guide to Genealogical and Historical Research.* Salt Lake City: Ancestry Publishing, 1990.

Newman, Debra L., comp. *Black History: A Guide to Civilian Records in the National Archives.* Washington, D.C.: National Archives Trust Fund Board: General Services Administration, 1984.

Phillips, Christopher. *Freedom's Port: The African American Community of Baltimore, 1790–1860.* Urbana: University of Illinois Press, 1997.

Roberts, Ralph. *Genealogy Via the Internet: Tracing Your Family Roots Quickly and Easily.* Alexander, North Carolina: Alexander Books, 1998.

Pope-Hennessy, James. *Sins of the Fathers: A Study of the Atlantic Slave Traders, 1441–1807.* New York: Alfred A. Knopf, 1968.

Rose, James, and Alice Eichholz. *Black Genesis.* Detroit: Gale Research Company, 1978.

Smith, Jessie Carney, ed. *Ethnic Genealogy: A Research Guide.* Westport, North Carolina and London: Greenwood Press, 1983.

Starobin, Robert S., ed. *Blacks in Bondage: Letters of American Slaves.* New York: New Viewpoints, 1974.

Still, William. *The Underground Rail Road.* 1872. Reprint, Chicago: Johnson Publishing Company, 1970.

Thomas, Hugh. *The Slave Trade: The Story of the Atlantic Slave Trade: 1440–1870.* New York: Simon & Schuster, 1997.

Thomas, Velma Maia. *Lest We Forget: The Passage From Africa to Slavery and Emancipation.* New York: Crown Publishers, Inc., 1997.

U.S. Department of Commerce: Bureau of the Census. *Historical Statistics of the United States: Colonial Times to 1970.* 2 vols. Washington, D.C., 1975.

———. *200 Years of U.S. Census Taking: Population and Housing Questions, 1790–1990.* Washington, D.C., 1989.

Ward, W. E. F. *The Royal Navy and the Slavers: The Suppression of the Atlantic Slave Trade.* New York: Pantheon Books, 1969.

Woodson, Carter G., ed. and comp. *A Century of Negro Migration*. 1918. Reprint, New York: AMS Press, Inc., 1970.

———. *Free Negro Owners of Slaves in the United States in 1830 Together With Absentee Ownership of Slaves in the United States in 1830*. 1924. Reprint, New York: Negro Universities Press, 1968.

Wright, Roberta Hughes, and Wilbur B. Hughes III. *Lay Down Body: Living History in African American Cemeteries*. Detroit: Visible Ink Press, 1996.

Index